ARDEN'S HOUSING LIBRARY

1

Series Editors: Andrew Arden QC and Caroline Hunter

Andrew Dymond is a practising barrister at Arden Chambers, specialising in housing, landlord and tenant, and local government law. He contributes articles on housing law to various legal journals and is a member of the Leasehold Enfranchisement Advisory Group.

SECURITY OF TENURE

Andrew Dymond

LEMOS ASSOCIATES
LONDON

Published in Great Britain 1995 by

Lemos Associates
20 Pond Square
London N6 6BA

Telephone 0181-348 8263

ISBN 1-898001-12-X

A CIP catalogue record for this book is
available from the British Library

Designed by Mick Keates
Phototypeset by Kerrypress Ltd, Luton
Printed by Redwood Books, Trowbridge

CONTENTS

TABLE OF CASES

TABLE OF STATUTES

INTRODUCTION

Security of tenure is the phrase used to describe the rights to remain in occupation which an occupier of property has against the owner of the property. The aim of this book is to provide a guide to security of tenure for those working in the management of social housing, in particular, housing managers and housing officers employed by local authorities and housing associations.

Security of tenure has been provided by a series of Acts of Parliament dating back to the early part of this century. In the public sector, security was introduced with the Housing Act 1980, which was later consolidated by the Housing Act 1985. Tenants who are given security of tenure under the 1985 Act are referred to as secure tenants.

The most significant subsequent piece of legislation is the Housing Act 1988. This replaced the Rent Act 1977, and provides that all residential tenancies created after 15 January 1989 are assured tenancies, except for those which are created by one of the public bodies which can create secure tenancies. Importantly, the Housing Act of 1988 also reduced the number of landlords capable of granting secure tenancies. Before 15 January 1989 tenancies granted by housing associations were governed by the regime of the Housing Act 1985. Indeed, tenancies granted before that date remained secure after the introduction of the Housing Act of 1988. Tenancies granted by housing associations after that date are assured tenancies.

Housing officers should also be familiar with the Protection from Eviction Act 1977, under which a person who grants a tenancy, or, in many cases even a licence, of a dwelling, to someone cannot evict that person without first obtaining a court order. Eviction without a court order is a criminal offence. Furthermore, the landlord may be liable to pay substantial damages to the person who has been unlawfully evicted.

Most of this book is concerned with the rights of tenants conferred by the Housing Acts of 1985 and 1988, which set out the two principal statutory codes which provide tenants of residential accommodation with security of tenure today. The importance of these statutes cannot, though, be understood without first comprehending the different ways in which someone may come to occupy property. Accordingly, the guide provides an introduction to the status of various types of occupier, as well as considering what constitutes a tenancy. Other matters, such as joint tenancies and subtenants, are also dealt with.

The main purpose of this book is to enable housing officers to identify:

- when a tenancy has been created;
- which Act applies to the tenancy;
- what rights to remain in the property (security of tenure) the tenant then has;
- how the security of tenure may be lost;

- which situations allow the landlord to terminate the tenancy;
- how the landlord is able to terminate the tenancy, and subsequently gain possession of the property.

The guide identifies the statutory framework within which a housing officer is working in a given case, demonstrating the options available to the officer in the management of a tenancy. Throughout the book examples are used to demonstrate the principles in a practical way. Many of these examples are real cases, although it has often been necessary to simplify the facts of each matter, and case references are provided.

CHAPTER 1

THE STATUS OF THE OCCUPIER

This book deals mainly with the relationship of landlord and tenant, since those employed by local authorities and housing associations, will usually be dealing with tenants. But it should be remembered that a tenant is only one of a number of types of occupier who may be encountered. Thus, someone may occupy a property as one of the following four types of occupier:

- owner occupier;
- tenant;
- licensee;
- trespasser.

Owner occupier

The term 'owner' may in some situations be misleading. The owner of the freehold of a house is clearly an owner occupier. Such a person has an interest in land which represents the strongest right of occupation.

Long Leaseholders

However, 'owner occupier' is also used to denote someone who does not own the freehold, but who has a long lease (commonly 99 or 125 years) which has been granted by the freeholder. Such an owner is, in law, only a type of tenant, but enjoys such control over the property that it is sensible to regard such a person as an owner occupier. These owner occupiers are often referred to as long leaseholders.

Almost all owners of flats are long leaseholders (although a new form of tenure for long leaseholders, called 'commonhold' is being proposed for the future). Usually, they have paid a substantial amount (a 'premium') to buy the long lease. During the term of the lease they pay a nominal rent, often called ground rent, to the freeholder. Providing the long leaseholder pays the ground rent, and does not breach any of the other terms of the lease, the leaseholder has a right to continue to live in the property for as long as the lease continues. Local authority housing officers often have to deal with long leaseholders who were formerly tenants, but who have purchased their homes under the 'right to buy'.

Rights to acquire freehold or extension of lease

Long leaseholders now have opportunities to obtain the freeholds of their properties. A full consideration of the rights which have been conferred is outside the ambit of this book. The following is only a brief summary of the legislation which applies in certain circumstances:

● A long leaseholder of a house has the right, under the Leasehold Reform Act 1967, to purchase the freehold, or compel the freeholder to grant him an extension of the lease.

● When the freeholder proposes to sell the freehold of a building divided into flats, he or she must, under the Landlord and Tenant Act 1987, first offer the freehold to the long leaseholders.

● A group of long leaseholders may, in certain circumstances, join together to compel their freeholder to sell them the freehold. This right arises from Part I of the Leasehold Reform, Housing and Urban Development Act 1993.

● A long leaseholder has the right, under Part II of the Leasehold Reform, Housing and Urban Development Act 1993, to compel the freeholder to grant an extension of the lease.

Tenant

The specific elements which must be present to constitute a tenancy are dealt with in the next chapter, but, in outline, if someone agrees to occupy a dwelling which is owned by someone else, and pays a regular rent to the owner, the owner of the property is a landlord and the other person is a tenant. In most cases, tenants are given protection by statute so that, as long as the tenant pays the rent, the landlord can evict the tenant only in certain limited circumstances.

Fixed term and periodic tenancies

There are two types of tenancy which are common: fixed term tenancies and periodic tenancies. Periodic tenancies are tenancies which are granted with reference to a specific period, normally a week or a month, and continue to run from week to week or month to month, as the case may be.

A fixed term tenancy, on the other hand, is granted for a specific period of time (eg, six months, or one year).

Written agreement

Neither type of tenancy must be set out in writing, although it is always desirable to draw up a written agreement for the obvious purpose of setting down the rights of the parties at the beginning of the tenancy. Fixed term tenancies for more than three years must, however, be in writing (section 53 of the Law of Property Act 1925).

Transfer or assignment of a tenancy

As well as being a contract, a tenancy is an interest in land. Consequently, it is capable of transfer or assignment to another person. All tenancies may be assigned, subject to the terms of the lease concerning assignment, and to statutory control. Assignment is usually by the formal mechanism of a deed, although a written document setting out the terms of the assignment will suffice under section 2 of the Law of Property (Miscellaneous Provisions) Act 1989.

Succession to a tenancy

As tenancies are interests in land they may be inherited on the tenant's death. A person who inherits a tenancy in this way is generally referred to as a successor. Whether statutory security of tenure applies to the successor depends on the statutory provisions. Generally on assignment and succession, see C. Hunter *Tenants' Rights* in Arden's Housing Library.

Joint tenants

If two or more people are tenants under an agreement, they are referred to as joint tenants. Similarly, there may be joint landlords if there is more than one landlord. The most common example of a joint tenancy is one held by cohabitees, often a husband and wife, although it should be remembered that others may be joint tenants. On the other hand, people who share the property in which they live are not necessarily joint tenants. Only those who were parties to the tenancy agreement itself are tenants. Indeed, technically, if one spouse alone was a party to the tenancy agreement, the other is no more than a licensee of the tenant (but see chapter 10). Where there is a written agreement, it may be presumed that the tenants are those who signed the agreement. But it is possible, depending on the circumstances, to demonstrate that the landlord was contracting with other parties in addition to the person or person(s) named as tenant(s) in the agreement.

To count as joint tenants each person must be able to establish the elements of a tenancy (exclusive occupation, at a term, for a rent). The essence of a joint tenancy is that each tenant has a right to use the whole of the property. A joint tenant cannot be said to own a specific share. Consequently, each joint tenant is liable for the whole rent of the property, so that, if one joint tenant abandons the property, the landlord may seek the entire rent from the remaining tenants.

Subtenants

Where the occupier of a premises is the tenant of someone who is in turn a tenant, then the occupier is called a subtenant. The occupier's landlord is often referred to as 'the mesne tenant'. The mesne tenant's landlord is referred to as the 'superior landlord'. The tenancy between the superior landlord and the mesne tenant is normally referred as the 'head tenancy' to distinguish it from the subtenancy. Of course, it is quite possible for there to be a series of subtenancies, creating what are termed 'intervening interests'.

The subtenant's relationship to the mesne tenant is simply that of landlord and tenant, as long as the mesne tenant's interest in the property continues. If the mesne tenant is a local housing authority, or another public sector landlord, then the subtenant will be a secure tenant. However, it may well be that the tenancy created by the local authority falls within one of the exceptions to a secure tenancy (see chapter 3, on development land and subleasing schemes). Similarly, if a housing association has been granted a lease of premises and sublets, the subtenants will be secure tenants or assured tenants, depending on the date the tenancy was created.

Licensee

The term 'licensee' covers a number of situations. Basically, a licensee is someone who has been given permission ('licence') to be on premises. The person who gives that permission is referred to as the licensor. An ordinary visitor – family friend or relative, doctor or social worker – is a licensee. Sometimes a licence is created by a contract. A person who pays money to be allowed onto property in certain circumstances – a member of a cinema audience, for instance – is a contractual licensee. As is evident from the examples given, a licensee has very limited rights to remain in the property following admission. Once the purpose for which the licensee was allowed onto the property has come to an end, the owner may remove the licensee.

Residential licence
Some occupiers of residential accommodation may be

licensees. The difference between being a residential licensee and a residential tenant is significant. A tenant has an interest which may, in certain circumstances, be assigned, or passed on to the family upon the death. As long as the tenant continues to live in the property, the landlord will be able to evict the tenant only in limited circumstances. A residential licensee on the other hand, can be evicted by the licensor with ease. If a notice in a particular form has been served on the licensee, there is no right to continue to remain in the property. For many years landlords tried to argue that they had granted licences rather than tenancies, and that the arrangements could be terminated with ease because the security of tenure afforded to tenants, but not to licensees, did not come into play. The distinction between a licence and a tenancy will be taken further in the next chapter. It is of particular significance to housing officers in the context of hostel accommodation, discussed below in chapter 10.

Trespasser

A trespasser is someone who occupies land without the owner's agreement or permission. He or she may previously have had permission to be on the property, or he or she may have entered the property without the knowledge of the owner. Such a person is often referred to as a squatter, or an unauthorised occupier, and has no security of tenure whatever. The owner of the land may remove a trespasser, as long as violence is not used. A fast method of obtaining possession against trespassers is provided by the courts.

Examples

A house, owned by Whittington Borough Council, is divided into four flats. Whittington Borough Council is the freeholder.

Flat 1

Mr Brown lives in flat 1. He purchased the flat under the 'right to buy' for £60,000, with the help of a mortgage, and has a 125 year lease. One of the rooms is occupied by Mr Chisholm who pays £45 a week to Mr Brown. For this Mr Chisholm has the use of one room, the kitchen and bathroom. Mr Brown cleans Mr Chisholm's room most days, changes his linen weekly, and can go into Mr Chisholm's room at any time. Mr Brown is an owner occupier (long leaseholder), and Mr Chisholm is a contractual licensee (lodger).

Flat 2

Mr and Mrs Davinski live in flat 2. In 1992 they signed an agreement with Whittington Borough Council, under which they pay £75 a week for the flat. Mr and Mrs Davinski are tenants of the flat, and, because they are both parties to the agreement, they are joint tenants. As we shall see in Chapter 3, they are secure tenants who have the security of tenure afforded by the Housing Act 1985.

Flat 3

Ms Elias owns flat 3 on a lease similar to Mr Brown's. She does not live there, but has let the flat to Ms Ferdinand who pays £125 a week for the use of the flat. Ms Elias is a home owner (long leaseholder), and Ms Ferdinand is her tenant.

Flat 4

Mr George lives in flat 4. Whittington Borough Council has no agreement with Mr George and has not given him permission to live there. Mr George is a trespasser.

CHAPTER 2

TENANT OR LICENSEE?

As has already been mentioned if an owner of property allows someone else to occupy that property, the occupier is either a tenant or a licensee. The difference can be crucial. A licensee usually has very limited rights to remain in the property if asked to leave, but a tenant will almost certainly have security of tenure, which means that the landlord can remove the tenant only in limited circumstances.

Elements of a tenancy

Certain conditions must be met for a tenancy to be created:

- There must be identifiable parties. The tenant does not have to know who the landlord is, but there must be a landlord and a tenant, who are two different entities. This requirement is rarely in dispute.
- There must be identifiable premises. As long as there is a defined space, a tenancy may be created. It may be as little

as one room or as much as a palace. Unless there are joint tenants, there cannot be a tenancy of premises which are shared with others.

• The arrangement must relate to a particular period of time. This is an essential requirement for a tenancy. With certain rare exceptions, a tenancy will either be for a fixed term (a 'fixed term' tenancy), or will refer to a particular period (a 'periodic' tenancy). A fixed term tenancy is stated to last for a particular time perhaps one year or six months. A periodic tenancy does not identify a definite date on which the tenancy will end, but specifies a period at the end of which a new period of the tenancy will commence, for example, a weekly or monthly tenancy.

• The occupier must have exclusive possession of the property. This is the vital distinction between a contractual licence and a tenancy of residential premises, and is considered further below.

Street v Mountford

As has already been noted it may be of great advantage to the owner of a property to argue that a licence rather than a tenancy has been created. Most cases concerning the difference between a tenancy and a licence have arisen because an owner has signed an agreement with an occupier which purports to be a licence agreement, when in reality the agreement was for a tenancy. In the case of *Street v Mountford* [1985] AC 809, the House of Lords stated that to determine whether or not a tenancy has been granted it is necessary to look not at the label given to the letting arrangement, but at the true substance of it, identifying whether or not the elements of a tenancy are present. If the occupier has exclusive possession of the premises for a term at a rent, then there is a presumption that a tenancy has been created.

It should be noted that the payment of rent alone does not establish that a tenancy has been created. It is merely one of the elements which the House of Lords identified as leading to the presumption that a tenancy had been created.

Exclusive possession

A contractual licensee also makes payments, and will do so with reference to a particular period. The crucial factor distinguishing a tenant from a licensee is exclusive possession. This is the right for the tenant to exclude others, including, most significantly, the owner, from the property. A tenant does not own the property in which he or she lives, but in all other ways that person may call the home their own. A lodger or licensee on the other hand, cannot do this because the owner needs to be able to enter the property, whether or not the occupier is there to give permission, to provide certain services. Examples of such services are room cleaning, removing rubbish, providing clean linen, and serving meals.

Sometimes a clause in the agreement will be incompatible with the grant of a licence. Thus, a clause under which an owner retains a right to enter the premises is inconsistent with a licence agreement because a licensor is able to enter the premises as of right and would not need a clause of this kind.

By way of exception, in the public sector, the Housing Act 1985 has provided security of tenure to a licensee (a 'secure tenant' is defined as someone to whom residential accommodation is let under a tenancy or a licence (section

79 of the Housing Act 1985). But the extension of security to licensees in this context has been limited. A licence can be secure only if it grants exclusive possession (*Westminster City Council v Clarke* (1992) 24 HLR 360 HL (see below)). This is very unlikely in practice since, if exclusive possession is granted, the agreement will normally create a tenancy.

Hostel accommodation

A common example of a licence agreement which housing officers may encounter arises in connection with hostel accommodation. The distinctive feature of much hostel accommodation is that its primary purpose is to provide housing and assistance to people who are for some reason vulnerable. They may be drug addicts, former prisoners, or the mentally ill. The hostel is provided to allow them to find their feet in society. It will normally have a resident housekeeper, and the attendant services, which have already been noted as the distinguishing feature of lodging agreements, will frequently be provided.

Terms

The licence agreement normally granted to occupiers of hostel rooms contains strict terms enabling the hostel managers to control and supervise the occupiers. The fact that the hostel retains the key to the occupier's room will not of itself necessarily mean that exclusive possession has not been granted; all the terms of the agreement would have to be considered to determine this question. The licence agreement usually limits the number of visitors an occupier may have and the times at which they may come. An occupier may be required to be in by a certain time at night unless permission to stay out later is given, and will be required to comply with the directions of the hostel manager or warden.

In the private sector, landlords who hoped to avoid security of tenure by granting sham licence agreements often included terms similar to these. Common examples were that the occupier would be required to move from one room in the premises to another at the request of the landlord, or would have to share a room with another person if so required. Such terms are often found in hostel agreements, and are genuinely included to facilitate the management of property where flexibility is required to accommodate a constant flow of people at different stages of rehabilitation, and in this context are therefore likely to be upheld as genuine. But in the context of privately rented accommodation these were plainly inconsistent with the grant of exclusive possession, and were struck down by the courts.

That is not to say that hostel accommodation cannot be let on tenancies, and security of tenure in hostels is considered further in Chapter 10.

Example

Mr Clarke lived in a hostel owned and managed by Westminster City Council. He was a vulnerable person, and the council had placed him in the hostel because he was homeless and the council was under a duty to provide him with accommodation. The hostel was for single men who had personality disorders and had been evicted from their previous homes, or who had been discharged from hospital or released from prison. There was a warden and a team of social workers who arranged resettlement of the occupiers. Mr Clarke had a licence agreement for his own room which included cooking facilities. The terms of the licence agreement allowed the council to move Mr Clarke from his room into another. The council terminated Mr Clarke's licence after he vandalised his room. The matter went to court and the Court of Appeal decided that Mr Clarke was a tenant. But on appeal, the House of Lords held that he was a licensee. He did not enjoy exclusive possession of his room. It was necessary to the running of the hostel for the council to retain possession of the rooms so that it could supervise and control the occupiers (*Westminster City Council v Clarke* (1992) 24 HLR 360).

Accommodation for the elderly

The discussion of hostel accommodation above applies also to accommodation for elderly people. Many such homes employ residential caretakers, and provide meals, changes of linen, and the other services which are typical of licence agreements. Furthermore, the agreements entered into by the residents often contain terms which are inconsistent with the granting of exclusive possession. The purpose of these terms is to facilitate the running of the home, and they are included because the granting of a tenancy would be incompatible with the home's purposes. Just as those running hostels require flexibility to cope with people at different stages of rehabilitation, so the managers of homes for the elderly need to be able to deal with, for example, residents whose health deteriorates to the extent that they should be moved to nursing homes where full-time medical attention can be provided.

Example

> Abbeyfield, a charity, ran a home for old people. Mr Woods entered into an agreement for one of the rooms at the home when he was 85. He made weekly payments for his unfurnished room, meals, heating, lighting, and a resident housekeeper. As part of the agreement, Abbeyfield reserved the right to take possession of the room, giving Mr Woods one month's notice, if it thought fit to do so. Abbeyfield stated that it would exercise this right only if it considered it 'absolutely essential in the interest of yourself and the other residents'. Sadly, Mr Woods deteriorated with age. He was blind and increasingly confused. Abbeyfield decided that he could no longer look after himself, and was a danger to himself and to other residents. Efforts were made to arrange accommodation for him in a nursing home, where he could be properly supervised and looked after, but Mr Woods refused to leave. The Court of Appeal upheld the decision of the county court judge that the agreement was for a licence and not a tenancy, in the light of the attendant services which were provided. Furthermore, in bringing the licence to an end, Abbeyfield had acted in good faith and reasonably, having had due regard to the interests of Mr Woods and the other residents (*Abbeyfield (Harpenden) Society Ltd v Woods* [1968] 1 WLR 374).

Exceptions where the three elements of a tenancy are present

In certain circumstances, although the occupier may have exclusive possession for a term at a rent, other factors may lead to the conclusion that a tenancy has not been created. In other words, the presumption that exclusive possession of property for a term at a rent creates a tenancy is rebutted. Examples are given below.

No intention to create legal relations

For a tenancy to come into existence there must be an intention to create a legal relationship between the parties. If an owner of property allows someone to stay in occupation because of, say, a family relationship, or as an act of charity, the relationship between the parties may lack this element.

The principle is important for those who manage housing if there has been a dispute between the parties to an earlier tenancy, or when money has been accepted from someone who is a stranger to the landlord. The problem often arises because the department which deals with the day-to-day management of the property may not be the same as that to which the rent is paid. The normal inference to be drawn from the payment and acceptance of rent is that a tenancy has been created, but if the landlord can show that the money was not accepted on the basis of an agreement for a tenancy (ie, that there was no intention to create legal relations between the parties), then the normal inference will not be made. The landlord will have to show that the payments were accepted by mistake, or by reference to a particular set of circumstances which demonstrate that there was no agreement to enter into a tenancy.

Examples

Westminster city council granted a tenancy to a married couple. In 1984 the wife left home, and Ms Basson moved in with the husband. This relationship in turn broke down and the man left in February 1985. The council noticed that Ms Basson was in the premises. They told her she had no right to remain, and that any money received from her would be damages for use and occupation of the premises. On 23 September 1985 the original tenancy was terminated by notice to quit. On 27 September the council wrote to Ms Basson reiterating their earlier advice. In particular, the letter stated 'In making payments as use and occupation charges this arrangement is not intended as the creation of a tenancy or a licence in any way whatsoever'. Ms Basson applied for rent rebate. She received various letters which assessed her rent rebate, and even stated that her tenancy had commenced on 23 September. In October 1986 possession proceedings were commenced. She was told that she would have to leave. In November 1987 possession proceedings were served on Ms Basson, even though she had been given a rent book in that year.

The judge held that no tenancy had been created, and the Court of Appeal upheld his decision. The occasional references to rent and a tenancy were incompatible with the possession proceedings which were afoot, and merely demonstrated that one department was unaware of the actions of another. There was no intention on the part of Westminster City Council to enter into a legal relationship.

This case demonstrates the confusion that may arise when a number of different departments deal with a particular tenancy, and the need for a clear letter to be written to the tenant explaining the local authority's position (*Westminster City Council v Basson* (1990) 23 HLR 225).

Basson was, however, distinguished in the following case.

In 1981 the GLC granted to Ms Ayinde's cousin and this cousin's husband (the cousins) a secure tenancy of a three bedroomed flat. In about late 1984, Ms Ayinde herself moved into the flat with her husband and three children. In about April 1985 the cousins moved back to Nigeria permanently. On 17 June, 1985, the cousins wrote to the GLC stating that they had moved and that they had agreed Ms Ayinde and her husband should take over the tenancy. The cousins wrote another letter to the GLC in July, purporting to transfer the tenancy to Ms Ayinde and her husband.

Following the dissolution of the GLC, Tower Hamlets Borough Council became the owners of the flat, in July 1985. On 29 May, 1986, one of the council's visiting officers went to the flat and told Ms Ayinde and her husband that they did not need any other housing and they could stay there. In October 1986 Ms Ayinde's husband died. During the following two years, she wrote about 20 letters and went to the council's offices many times, requesting that the tenancy be transferred into her name. Only one of the letters, sent in February or March 1987, was retained by the council. In that letter Ms Ayinde stated she was a tenant and asked for the facility to pay her rent directly from her wages.

From September 1988 onwards Ms Ayinde was regarded by the council as an unlawful occupier, although they did not tell her so. On 8 June 1990, they wrote to her enclosing a notice to quit purporting to determine the cousins' tenancy. From the time of her husband's death Ms Ayinde had paid the rent for the premises, and it had been accepted by the council in the knowledge that it was paid on her own behalf.

In January 1992 the council commenced possession proceedings. At the trial, the judge found that there had been a surrender of the cousins' tenancy by operation of law, and the grant of a new tenancy to Ms Ayinde. The

Court of Appeal upheld this decision. Not only had the cousins' tenancy been surrendered (see chapter 12), but there had been a clear grant of a new tenancy to Ms Ayinde. A landlord who had received a letter such as the one Ms Ayinde had sent, and had continued, without protest, to accept payments, could not deny that she had been accepted as a tenant (*London Borough of Tower Hamlets v Ayinde* (1994) 26 HLR).

Tied accommodation

Many large employers, including local authorities, provide accommodation for their employees. Often the contract of employment refers to the accommodation, and specifies that the right for the employee to remain in the accommodation will come to an end at the same time as the job comes to an end. Caretakers, resident housekeepers, and pub managers are obvious examples of people who are provided with accommodation along with their jobs.

Service occupiers and service tenants

Such an employee is known as a service resident and may be a tenant or a licensee. A service licensee is termed a 'service occupier', whereas one who is a tenant is called a 'service tenant'. A service resident may not be a tenant because that person does not enjoy exclusive occupation, but there is a further test which may prevent a service resident from becoming a tenant.

Accommodation essential for the job

Essentially, a distinction is drawn between accommodation which is provided because it is vital to the performance of the job (as in the case of a caretaker responsible for the 24-hour running of a housing estate, or school), and accommodation which is provided as a form of benefit with the job.

The test is in two stages:

● Is it, in fact, 'necessary' to live in the accommodation provided to be able to carry out the job? If the answer is yes then the resident is a service occupier. If no, it is necessary to go on to look at the contract of employment.

● Does the contract state that the employee is required as part of the employment to live in the property, and is that requirement imposed for the better performance of the job? If the answer is yes, the employee is a service occupier. However, the term of the contract must be genuine; it cannot be included by the landlord merely to deny the employee the security of tenure which would otherwise apply. The fact that it is convenient for the employee to reside in the property does not make the agreement for the better performance of duties. Whether or not the requirement is genuine depends on the facts of each case.

Rights of the employee
The difference is significant. A service occupier has no right to remain in the property after the employment has expired. A service tenant enjoys whatever security of tenure would be afforded, depending on who the landlord is. Furthermore, tenants enjoy various ancillary rights, for example, secure tenants have the right to buy the premises let to them. However, there are certain specific grounds for possession in the Housing Acts of both 1985 and 1988. These are considered in chapters 7 and 8.

A service occupier may argue that although the contract of employment has been terminated, there is a claim for unfair dismissal pending in an industrial tribunal, and that an order for possession should not therefore be made until the outcome of the tribunal proceedings is known. However, an employer is not obliged to reinstate someone who has been unfairly dismissed, and, if the landlord has already engaged a replacement, the industrial tribunal would probably not consider it reasonable to order reinstatement.

Examples

> Mr Griffiths was a caretaker who worked for a school run by a local authority. When he started his job, he already lived in council accommodation, although, obviously, this was not connected with his employment. In 1956 the council bought a house next to the school for the caretaker to live in, and Mr Griffiths moved in. In 1976 South Glamorgan County Council became the education authority for the area. They provided Mr Griffiths with a statement of his duties which included a term that 'it shall be a condition of employment that a caretaker must reside in school accommodation where such premises are available'. In 1990 it was decided that the school should be closed. In May 1990 Mr Griffiths was told that possession of the house would be required. In July 1990 Mr Griffiths retired, and in the same month an invalid notice to quit was served. A valid notice to quit was served in August 1990. Although the term quoted above had not been included in Mr Griffith's original contract of employment, which prevailed when he moved into the home, the judge held that there were clear grounds for implying the term into the tenancy agreement of a caretaker's contract.

Alternatively, Mr Griffiths argued that he had retired in July 1990, but that a valid notice to quit had not been served until August. In the interim he had become a secure tenant, because he was not a service occupier during this time, and had exclusive possession for a term at a rent. This argument was rejected. His occupation of the house continued to relate to his employment. There was no agreed or intended change in the nature and purposes of his occupation of the premises. The Court of Appeal dismissed Mr Griffiths's appeal (*South Glamorgan County Council v Griffiths* (1992) 24 HLR 334).

Mr Hughes was a headmaster employed by an education authority. In 1961 the authority built a home for the headmaster in the school grounds. Mr Hughes' contract did not specify that he was required to occupy the house for the better performance of his duties. The case went all the way to the House of Lords. It was held that the term 'for the better performance of duties' would be implied into a contract of employment only if it could be demonstrated that occupation of the property was essential to the better performance of the job. There was no evidence that the job could not have been done equally well if the headmaster lived in another house. It was not essential for him to live in the house in the school grounds. Accordingly, he was a secure tenant of the house (*Hughes v Greenwich London Borough Council* [1994] 1 AC 170).

If the landlord is unable to establish that an employee is a service occupier, the fact that a tenant is an employee may give the landlord extra rights to possession. With regard to secure tenancies reference should be made to paragraphs 2 and 5 of Schedule 1 to the Housing Act 1985 (service occupiers cannot be secure tenants; job mobility accommodation), grounds 7 (employee guilty of conduct incompatible with the use of the building) and 12 (termination of employment). With regard to assured tenancies, ground 16, set out in Schedule 2 to the Housing Act 1988, provides a basis for possession when a tenancy is let in consequence of a contract of employment and that employment has ceased. The tenant may of course be moved from the property before the termination of employment if suitable alternative accommodation is available and the court considers it reasonable to make an order for possession (ground 9H of the same Schedule). These grounds are considered in chapters 6 and 7.

CHAPTER 3

SECURE AND ASSURED TENANCIES

Security of tenure for tenants of social landlords is governed by the Housing Acts of 1985 and 1988. Tenants protected by the Housing Act 1985 are referred to as secure tenants, while tenants protected by the 1988 Act are called assured tenants. Although elements of the Acts are common to both types of tenancy, the difference is crucial. In broad terms, secure tenancies are granted by landlords in the public sector, and tenancies created by other landlords are assured. In the case of housing association tenants, the date of the tenancy agreement is significant. Tenancies created by housing associations on or after 15 January 1989 are assured, those created before that date are secure (section 35(4) of the Housing Act 1988). To establish the regime which applies to a particular case, it is necessary first to decide the category into which the landlord falls, and then to check that the tenancy does not come within one of the exceptions contained in the Schedules to the Acts.

Secure tenancies: the landlord condition

A tenancy can be a secure tenancy under the Housing Act 1985 only if it was granted by one of the landlords who are capable of granting secure tenancies. The introduction of the Housing Act 1988 complicated the position with regard to certain landlords (most notably housing associations). If the interest of the landlord is jointly owned, all the joint owners must be bodies who qualify as secure landlords for the tenancy to be secure.

The 'landlord condition' is satisfied if the landlord is one of the following (section 80 of the 1985 Act):
- a local authority;
- a new town corporation;
- a housing action trust;
- an urban development corporation;
- the Development Board for Rural Wales;

If the tenancy was entered into before 15 January 1989 (the date the Housing Act 1988 came into force), the landlord condition is also fulfilled if the landlord is:
- the Housing Corporation;
- a housing trust which is a charity;
- a housing association to which section 80 of the Housing Act 1985 formerly applied.

Section 80 applied to a registered housing association (ie, registered with the Housing Corporation) unless the association was a co-operative housing association (ie, a fully mutual housing association registered under the Industrial and Provident Societies Act 1965). It also applied to an unregistered housing association which was a co-operative housing association at the relevant time.

If the landlord is the Housing Corporation, a charitable housing trust, or a relevant housing association, the key date is the commencement of the tenancy. A tenancy or licence granted by such a landlord before 15 January 1989 will be secure. A tenancy but not a licence granted on or after that date will be assured. Licensees of landlords in this category have no security of tenure if the licence was granted on or after 15 January 1989. Such a licence may be brought to an end by serving a notice to quit.

Furthermore, the effect of section 35 of the Housing Act 1988 is to be noted. A tenant of a housing association who has a secure tenancy will remain a secure tenant if:

● the tenant is transferred to another property owned by the same association; or

● the tenant is granted a tenancy of a different property because a possession order has been made against him or her on the basis that the different property is suitable alternative accommodation, and the court directed that the new tenancy would be a housing association tenancy (see further Schedule 2 to the Housing Act 1985 grounds 9 to 16; and chapters 6 and 8).

Managing agents

Often the day-to-day running of property is undertaken not by the landlord, but by managing agents. The fact that the landlord uses managing agents does not affect the landlord condition. It is the identity of the landlord, and not the managing agents, which determines whether a tenancy is assured or secure.

Exceptions: tenancies which are not secure

Although the landlord condition may be satisfied, the tenancy may still not be secure. Schedule 1 to the Housing Act 1985 contains 12 paragraphs setting out the list of exceptions.

Long leases (paragraph 1)

Leases for more than 21 years are excluded, ie owner occupiers are not secure tenants. Thus, when a secure tenant has exercised the right to buy, they cease to be secure.

Employee accommodation (paragraph 2)

This exception means that service occupiers, as opposed to service tenants, do not receive security of tenure under the Housing Act 1985. Premises occupied under a contract of employment which requires the tenant to occupy the dwelling-house for the better performance of duties are excepted if the tenant is an employee of the landlord, or of one of the following:

- a local authority;
- a new town development corporation;
- the Commission for New Towns;
- a county council;
- the Development Board for Rural Wales;
- an urban development corporation or a housing action trust.

In addition, premises provided to police officers free of rent and rates under the Police Act 1964 are excepted. So too are premises rented to fire fighters, in consequence of their employment, where their contracts of employment require them to live close to a particular station. There are also provisions which prevent lettings of premises which fall within the above exceptions in the previous three years from being secure, even where the tenant is not in the requisite employment. Such a tenant must be notified in writing, before the tenancy begins, that the exception applies.

Development land (paragraph 3)

Premises on land acquired for development which is being used pending development for temporary housing are excluded. The type of tenancy which arises here is often referred to as 'short-life user', although some major developments may take many years before the works are commenced, and a letting of several years may still be temporary. In *Attley v Cherwell DC* (1989) 21 HLR 613, the tenants had been granted a fixed term tenancy of ten years. The letting was held still to fall within the exception.

'Development' is defined in section 55(1) of the Town and Country Planning Act 1990 as 'the carrying out of building, engineering, mining, or other operations in, on, and over or under land, or the making of any material change in the use of the buildings or other land'. Change of use includes the conversion of a house into flats. If a change in circumstances leads to an alteration in the plans, the exception will still apply, see *Attley v Cherwell DC*, above. If, however, development plans are subsequently rejected, with the result that there is no pending development, the exception will cease to apply. It is not necessary for the landlord to be the one who acquired the land for development.

Examples

> Hyde Housing Association held a flat under an agreement with the Department of Transport under which the housing association could use the flat to provide temporary accommodation. The Department of Transport had acquired the flat to enable it to carry out a future road development scheme. In 1984, the housing association had granted a licence to Mr Harrison. The Court of Appeal held that the licence was not a secure tenancy, because paragraph 3 of Schedule 2 to the 1985 Act applied. The dwelling-house was on land acquired for development, and was being used by the landlord, pending the development of the land, as temporary housing accommodation (*Hyde Housing Association Ltd v Harrison* (1990) 23 HLR 57).

Lambeth Borough Council had acquired certain houses under a compulsory purchase order in 1971. The houses were originally to be demolished, but in 1978 the council decided instead to improve them. In 1981 the council entered into a licence agreement with a housing association, which in turn sub-licensed the houses to Lillieshall Road Housing Co-operative. Mr Brennan was granted a license by the co-operative to occupy one of the houses. In 1990 the co-operative sought to evict him on the basis that the licence was not secure, as paragraph 3 applied to it. The evidence from the council was that development proposals had been rejected by the Department of the Environment as too costly, and that currently the council might keep the property as a family house without any development, or might convert it into two or more separate dwellings. The Court of Appeal held that there was no evidence on which it could be said that development was still pending in relation to the land (*Lillieshall Road Housing Co-op Ltd v Brennan* (1991) 24 HLR 195).

Accommodation for homeless persons (paragraph 4)

Local authorities owe a duty to house certain homeless persons. In some situations the duty is to provide temporary accommodation only. If such temporary accommodation is provided, the tenancy is not secure for the first year after it is granted, unless the landlord notifies the tenant that a secure tenancy is to be granted.

The three relevant duties to the homeless are:
- to house pending inquiries in case of apparent priority need (section 63 of the Housing Act 1985);
- to house temporarily a person found to have priority need but to have become homeless intentionally (section 65(3) of the Housing Act 1985);
- to house while considering whether or not to refer the

applicant to another housing authority (section 68(1) of the Housing Act 1985).

In either of the first two cases, the twelve months run from the date on which the authority gives written notice of its decision to the applicant. In the third case, it runs from the date the authority notifies the applicant of the decision of the two authorities.

Example

> Mr Walsh applied to Eastleigh Borough Council as homeless. Pending a decision on the application, he was offered the tenancy of a house, and moved in October 1981. His wife and children either never moved into the house or did so and then moved out very soon afterwards, but Mr Walsh did not inform the council of this, and the council did not become aware of it until July 1982. On 15 July 1982 the council wrote to Mr Walsh that he did not qualify for assistance under the homeless persons provisions as he had no dependants. They also invited him to vacate the house.
>
> Although no notice to quit was served on Mr Walsh, the council commenced possession proceedings in February 1983, on the basis that he was only a licensee. Mr Walsh defended on the basis that he was a tenant, and that due to the elapse of 12 months, the tenancy had become secure. In the House of Lords it was held that a tenancy had been granted, the council had failed to terminate the tenancy by service of a notice to quit and consequently the tenancy had become secure 12 months from the date of the letting (*Eastleigh Borough Council v Walsh* [1985] 1 WLR 525).

Job mobility accommodation (paragraph 5)

This exception applies to temporary accommodation granted to a person who was not formerly a resident in the district or London Borough where the accommodation is situated. The purpose of the tenancy must be to enable the tenant to take up employment or an offer of employment within that district or London Borough, or within an adjoining district or London Borough, while looking for permanent accommodation. Before the grant of the tenancy the landlord must notify the tenant that the exception applies. It applies for one year, or less if, during that year, the landlord notifies the tenant that he or she is to become a secure tenant.

Subleasing schemes (paragraph 6)

The pressures on public sector housing have made this an important exception, particularly for local authorities housing the homeless. This scheme is often referred to as short term leasing or private sector leasing. The landlord takes a lease from an owner of private sector premises. This may be of great benefit to an owner of property wishing to derive an income from letting the property without the worries of letting directly to an assured tenant. Local authorities have found that such subleasing schemes are useful for them in discharging their duties to the homeless, for they can avoid the problems inherent in creating a temporary housing agreement under paragraph 4 (see above), which, of course, becomes a secure tenancy after a year.

There is normally a fixed term lease between the owner and the housing authority, but, it is permissible to use a lease on the basis that it will terminate when required by the superior landlord. It is also permissible for the agreement between the superior landlord and the local authority to be a licence: *London Borough of Tower Hamlets v Miah* (1991) 24 HLR 199 (CA). The local authority then grants a subtenancy, or a licence, which is not secure.

It may be that the housing authority requires possession of the premises before its duties to the occupier have been fulfilled. Often this will be because the lease is coming to an end and the authority needs to give the property back to the owner with vacant possession. If the authority has a duty to house the occupier, it may be that the occupier does not want to move to the new premises offered, saying they are unsuitable. This is no defence to a possession action. The occupier may, though, have a remedy by way of judicial review of the housing authority landlord, arguing that the offer of the new property is one that no reasonable authority could make. All that the tenant could achieve by this would be an adjournment of the possession action pending the judicial review.

Accommodation pending works (paragraph 7)
A tenancy granted to a non-secure tenant (for example, someone who falls within one of the exceptions now being considered or a tenant of a private sector landlord) while works are carried out to the tenant's regular home is not a secure tenancy. This exception enables local authorities to offer temporary housing to private sector tenants to facilitate improvements to their homes, if the private sector landlord is unwilling or unable to provide the temporary accommodation. (With regard to works on the premises of a secure tenant see ground 10 of Schedule 2 to the Housing Act 1985 for removing the tenant while works are carried out, and ground 8 for requiring the tenant to return to the premises once the works are completed. These are considered in chapter 6.)

Agricultural holdings (paragraph 8)

Licensed premises (paragraph 9)

Student lettings (paragraph 10)
A letting to a student to enable the tenant to attend a des-

ignated course (ie designated by the Secretary of State) at
an educational establishment is not a secure tenancy if the
landlord notifies the student, before granting the tenancy,
that the exception applies. The exception ceases if the landlord notifies the student that he or she is to become a secure
tenant. The tenant remains non-secure until six months
after he or she ceases to attend the educational establishment, or, if the tenant fails to take up their place on the
course, six months after the grant of the tenancy.

Business lettings (paragraph 11)
Business tenancies are not within the ambit of the Housing
Act 1985. A property let for business purposes, but which
is used as a home, will not become subject to a secure tenancy because the property was not let 'as a [separate]
dwelling' (see chapter 4: residence condition). In contrast,
a secure tenant may lose security under the Act if the main
use of the premises becomes the conduct of a business.
Taking in lodgers is not a business for this purpose. This
issue will always be a question of fact and degree. The distinction to be drawn is between a business which is merely incidental, and a business which may be said to have
become the main reason for the tenant's occupation of the
property. Business tenancies have their own form of security of tenure under Part II of the Landlord and Tenant Act
1954.

Almshouses (paragraph 12)

Assured tenancies

If a tenancy is granted by a landlord other than one who
can grant a secure tenancy, then, if it is granted on or after

15 January 1989, it will be an assured tenancy under the Housing Act 1988. Schedule 1 to the Act sets out a long list of exceptions to this general rule not all of which are relevant here. Certain exceptions are common to both the Housing Act 1985 and the Housing Act 1988. These include agricultural holdings, business lettings and licensed premises. Exceptions under the 1988 Act which are of particular interest are considered next.

Exceptions: tenancies which are not assured

Tenancies created before the commencement of the Act (paragraph 1)

A tenancy which was entered into before, or pursuant to a contract made before, the commencement of the Housing Act 1988 (15 January 1989) cannot be an assured tenancy. In the private sector, the Rent Act 1977 will apply. Housing association tenancies created before this date will be secure tenancies under the Housing Act 1985.

Tenancies of premises with high rateable values (paragraph 2)

Accommodation of high value does not qualify for the protection of the Housing Act 1988. To be outside the remit of the Act the premises must have a rateable value greater than £1,500 if the premises are in Greater London; £750 elsewhere. In the case of a flat, the relevant rateable value is that of the part of the premises, ie the flat, occupied by the tenant, not the whole building.

If the tenancy was granted after 1 April 1990, and the property had not been assigned a rateable value on 31 March 1990, the tenancy will be excluded if the rent is more than £25,000 a year.

Long leaseholders (paragraph 3)

As in the case of secure tenancies, owner occupiers are excluded from protection. The criterion is the amount of the annual rent (usually referred to as 'ground rent'). If the annual ground rent is less than two-thirds of the rateable value of the premises, the tenancy is excluded. If the tenancy was granted after 1 April 1990, and there was no rateable value for the property on 31 March 1990, it will be excluded if the rent is £1,000 a year or less in Greater London, or £250 or less elsewhere.

Business tenancies (paragraph 4)

As under the Housing Act 1985, business tenancies are not protected (see above, page 38).

Licensed premises (paragraph 5)

As under the Housing Act 1985, licensed premises are not protected.

Tenancies of agricultural land (paragraph 6)

Tenancies of agricultural holdings (paragraph 7)

Student lets (paragraph 8)

A tenancy will not be assured if the landlord is one of a number of specified (ie, specified by the Secretary of State) educational institutions and the tenant is pursuing or intends to pursue a course of study at the landlord's institution, or at another of the specified institutions (see also page 37).

Holiday lets (paragraph 9)

Holiday homes are excluded. Landlords have resorted to sham holiday letting agreements in attempts to avoid security of tenure. This exception is of little interest in the context of social housing.

Resident landlords (paragraph 10)

Paragraph 10 of the Schedule excludes from security cases in which there is a resident landlord. There are complex provisions about the meaning of a 'resident landlord', but the exception cannot apply in the case of a housing association, since the landlord has to be an individual. Thus, the fact that a member of staff lives in a flat in a converted house belonging to a housing association which lets other flats in the building to other people, will not bring a housing association within the exception.

Crown tenancies (paragraph 11)

If the landlord is the Crown, or, more relevantly, a government department, the tenancy is excluded from the provisions of the Housing Act 1988. Tenancies under the management of the Crown Estate Commissioners do not fall into this exception.

The National Health Service and Community Care Act 1990 also reduced the Crown's immunity. A tenancy created by the NHS, or an NHS trust, after 1 April 1991 will be an assured tenancy. As such tenancies will generally have been granted to employees, the landlord will have recourse to ground 16 of Schedule 2 to the 1988 Act; see chapter 6.

Exempt landlords (paragraph 12)

This paragraph exempts the landlords who can create secure tenancies only (see above).

Tenants with other classes of protection (paragraph 13)

Secure tenants, or protected tenants under the Rent Act 1977 cannot be assured tenants, thus preserving their existing status.

Homeless persons (section 1(6), (7), Housing Act 1988)
See the similar exception under the 1985 Act, page 34. The exception under the 1988 Act concerns the same homeless persons to whom the local authority owes a limited duty. If the authority has provided temporary accommodation through another landlord for the initial period of one year, the tenancy will not be assured, unless the landlord notifies the tenant to the contrary.

Change of landlord

The buyer of a property takes the property subject to the rights of any tenants who may be occupying it. Consequently, before property is sold, the seller is normally required to reveal to the buyer any other interests, which will include tenancies, in the property. On a transfer of property, special considerations arise in relation to secure tenants.

Current government policy is to reduce public sector housing. Part III of the Housing Act 1988 introduced Housing Action Trusts (HATs) to take over housing stock in certain areas in place of, or in conjunction with, the local housing authority. Part IV of the same Act introduced 'tenant's choice', under which tenants can require a public sector landlord to transfer housing stock to an approved landlord (normally a housing association). HATs are themselves included in the list of landlords who create secure tenancies, and, accordingly, tenants will remain secure on transfer of the landlord's interest to a HAT. Housing associations now grant assured tenancies, and so tenants who exercise tenant's choice will become assured tenants on transfer.

CHAPTER 4

CONDITIONS FOR SECURITY OF TENURE

Security of tenure has evolved to give tenants a measure of certainty that they will be able to stay in their houses. If the premises let are not used as a home then security of tenure is lost. It is not the purpose of the security of tenure provisions to enable people to profit by subletting, or to benefit of those who have other homes. Both Acts require the tenant to live in the premises in question. This is known as the 'residence condition' and must be satisfied for the tenant to enjoy security of tenure. The Acts also specify other requirements to be met before security is afforded to the occupier.

Secure tenancy

The following requirements must be satisfied for there to be a secure tenancy (sections 79 and 81 of the Housing Act 1985):

- there must be a tenancy or a licence which grants exclusive possession (*Westminster City Council v Clarke* (1992) 24 HLR 360, (HL),
- of a dwelling-house,
- which is let or licensed as a separate dwelling;
- the tenant must be an individual (not a company);
- the tenant must occupy the premises as his or her only or principal home.

Assured tenancy

The following requirements must be satisfied for there to be an assured tenancy (section 1 of the Housing Act 1988):
- there must be a tenancy (not a licence),
- of a dwelling-house,
- which is let as a separate dwelling;
- the tenant must be an individual (not a company);
- the tenant must occupy the premises as his or her only or principal home.

'Dwelling-house'

This is a general term which embraces all accommodation. Houses and flats are included, and a single room can constitute a dwelling-house. Depending on the circumstances, a caravan could be considered a dwelling-house if it has been rendered completely immobile. Otherwise, mobile homes have their own, limited, security of tenure under the Mobile Homes Act 1983.

'Let as a separate dwelling'

Each component of this phrase requires examination.

'As' indicates that the purpose of the letting must be established. If the landlord lets a set of rooms for use 'as' an office, the tenant cannot subsequently use them for residential purposes without the knowledge and consent of the landlord and claim the protection of the Act. If the landlord does consent to change the use of the premises to residential purposes then security will be gained.

The premises must be occupied as 'a' single dwelling.

'Separate'

The dwelling must be 'separate', in that it must be capable of use as a complete dwelling in its own right. There must be no need to share essential living accommodation. 'Essential living accommodation', however, has been held not to include a bathroom. Otherwise, the tenancy must comprise a room or rooms where all the primary living activities, ie, sleeping, cooking and eating, may be conducted. The absence of a cooker in the premises may not be fatal. The tenant may simply be someone who chooses not to cook. If it can be shown that cooking could take place, ie that it would be possible to install cooking facilities, then the tenancy may still be of a separate dwelling.

Shared accommodation

Although the dwelling-house must be let as a separate dwelling, those who live in shared accommodation are nevertheless assured tenants under the Housing Act 1988. This situation might arise in a hostel, where there are shared kitchen and living rooms. Section 3 of the 1988 Act provides that where a tenant shares essential living accommodation with others (except for the landlord) he or she will still be an assured tenant.

There is no equivalent of section 3 in the 1985 Act. Accordingly, tenants who share accommodation with other tenants cannot be secure tenants. The shared use of a bathroom or lavatory will not take the tenancy out of the ambit of the Act, but a tenant who shares a kitchen will not have security of tenure. Most public sector residential tenants are not affected by this requirement, but it does mean that some hostel dwellers cannot be secure, even where they have exclusive possession of their own rooms. The implications of this are considered further in chapter 10.

Use as a home: the residence condition

Common to both Acts is the requirement that tenants occupy the premises as their 'only or principal home'. Some tenants will take a great deal of care in decorating and furnishing their homes; others may choose to have few possessions, and may not even spend a great deal of time at home. The word 'home' signifies different things to different people. In general, a home is the place where a person carries out the normal activities of sleeping, eating, cooking, and receiving friends. Some tenants, however, may never entertain friends at home; others may never cook, preferring to eat in cafés or make do with take-aways, others may rarely sleep at home. For a dwelling to be someone's home, there must be a 'substantial degree of regular personal occupation by the tenant of an essentially personal nature' (*Herbert v Byrne* [1964] 1 WLR 519). The question is whether the tenant can be said to use the dwelling-house as a home, or as a mere convenience. For it to be called a home, a property must be more than just an address from which the tenant collects the mail, or where the tenant occasionally sleeps or stores belongings. Whether or not the property is used as a home is a question of fact and degree in each case.

The following example concerns a 'resident landlord', ie, a landlord who lives in the same building as the tenant. The resident landlord is rarely encountered by social landlords, and so is not considered at length in this book, but the test of residence is the same for a landlord as for a tenant. Tenants of resident landlords do not have security of tenure under the Housing Act 1988. To qualify as a resident landlord, the landlord must demonstrate that he or she has occupied the dwelling as his or her only or principal home. The following case is included as an analogy, because the landlord in this case neither cooked nor slept at the premises, and cooking and sleeping in the premises are often considered essential if a dwelling is to be considered a home.

Example

Mr Palmer owned a flat. He granted Mr McNamara a tenancy of the front room of the flat, which contained a kitchen diner. Mr Palmer occupied and kept his belongings in the back room. The bathroom was to be shared between them. Mr Palmer spent every day in the back room, but he did not have any cooking facilities there. When he wished to eat he bought food which did not require cooking, or take-aways. He had a medical condition which prevented him from dressing himself. Accordingly, he never slept in the back room, but, instead, spent each night at a friend's house. The county court judge held that Mr Palmer did occupy the premises as his only or principal home, and made a possession order against Mr McNamara on the basis that he did not have any security of tenure. The Court of Appeal upheld the judge's

> decision. Just because Mr Palmer chose not to cook at the premises did not mean that the room he occupied could not qualify as a dwelling-house. It would have been possible for Mr Palmer to have a cooker installed if he had so wished. It was a question of fact and degree whether a person occupied a dwelling as his only or principal home (*Palmer v McNamara* (1990) 23 HLR 168).

Absence from the premises

The tenant may appear to have left or abandoned the property. A tenant cannot, of course, be expected to be in the property 24 hours a day. Conversely, a tenant who really has left the dwelling for good will lose security of tenure. Tenants may be away for long periods, on holiday, or in hospital, for instance. The tenant's employment may entail being away from home. In such circumstances the residence condition is still clearly satisfied. A tenant may have left the property because of a matrimonial dispute, or even domestic violence. Here it will be a question of fact whether an intention to return to the property can be established. (For the possibility of one joint tenant terminating the joint tenancy in cases involving matrimonial disputes, see chapter 12.) There is a large body of case-law on when an absence can be said to be so prolonged that the residence condition is no longer satisfied.

Prolonged absence

Once a tenant has been absent for a sufficient length of time, the tenant must, to establish that residence continues, demonstrate:
- an intention to return (the subjective element);
- visible signs in the property which are evidence of the intention to return (the objective element).

In practice, it is this objective element which the tenant will have difficulty in proving, but, if the subjective intention to return is absent, the fact that the tenant satisfies the objective test will not suffice. Normally, the tenant will be able to rely on personal possessions, in particular furniture, decorations, clothes, books and records, left in the premises to demonstrate the intention to return. Alternatively, someone, a partner or a friend, may remain in the property, occupying it on the tenant's behalf. It will be a question of fact whether the occupier occupies on the tenant's behalf, or the reality of the situation is that the tenant has left, and allowed the occupier to live in the dwelling. The tenancy will cease to be secure/assured if someone other than the tenant is in occupation and the tenant does not in fact intend to return.

The tenant's absence may be lengthy, it may run to a number of years, but this will not defeat a genuine intention to return and objective evidence of that intention. Reasons for absence which have been accepted by the court include being away on business; quitting the premises temporarily because they have deteriorated to such an extent that they are uninhabitable; spending time in hospital (provided the illness is not incurable); and looking after relatives.

In the case of a joint tenancy it is not necessary for all the tenants to occupy the premises as their only or principal home for the residence condition to be satisfied. Only one of the joint tenants has to satisfy the condition. This is true of both secure and assured tenancies (section 81 of the 1985 Act and section 1of the 1988 Act).

Two homes

It is not necessary for the dwelling-house to be the tenant's only home; the residence condition is satisfied if it is the principal home. Nevertheless, the courts will be reluctant to give security of tenure to a tenant who spends a great deal of time living elsewhere. The reason for the tenant's absence is all important. A tenant may be away from home to take care of relatives during illness, or while embarking on a relationship, and yet the intention to return will remain. Which of two homes is the tenant's principal home is a question of fact.

Examples

Mr Green, a tenant, left his home to care for his sick parents. He left his furniture, books, records, and some clothes in his home. He stayed with his parents for two years, looking after them. After they died, he stayed on to organise the sale of their home. He always intended to return to his own home, and while he was away he allowed two friends to live there periodically. Despite the length of Mr Green's absence, he could demonstrate both a subjective intention to return, and evidence of continued occupation (ie, his belongings, and occupation by his friends). He did not lose security of tenure (*Richards v Green* (1983) 11 HLR 1).

Mr Sawyer was granted a secure tenancy of a property by Crawley Borough Council in 1985. During the same year he went to live with his girlfriend. Subsequently the gas and electricity supplies to the property were cut off. In May 1986 The council learned that the property was vacant. In July 1986 Mr Sawyer told the council that he was living with his girlfriend, and they intended to buy her home. In August 1986 the council gave Mr Sawyer notice to quit the property. By that time his relationship had broken up, and he returned to live in the property in October 1986, after the notice to quit had expired. During the period of his absence he had paid the rent and rates for the property, visited it once a month, and at one stage had spent a week there. He said he intended to return to the property and had not abandoned it. The judge held that the premises were Mr Sawyer's principal home, and did not make a possession order. The Court of Appeal upheld his decision (*Crawley Borough Council v Sawyer* (1988) 20 HLR 98).

A tenant of a housing association was convicted of murdering his lover and sentenced to life imprisonment. The Home Office said he was likely to spend at least ten years in prison before he could be considered for parole. He left a relative in his flat who paid his rent. In an unreported county court decision on these facts, it was held that the tenant continued to be a secure tenant.

Subletting and lodgers

Secure tenants have an absolute right to take in lodgers as long as the property does not become statutorily overcrowded. A secure tenant may also sublet part of the property if the landlord gives its consent. (See further, C. Hunter *Tenants' Rights*, Arden's Housing Library.)

Loss of security of tenure

If a secure tenant sublets the whole of the property, then the residence condition is no longer satisfied. Even where the tenant resumes occupation after the subletting that person cannot regain the status of a secure tenant, which was lost because of the subletting (section 93(2) of the Housing Act 1985).

Whether or not an assured tenant is able to sublet part of the property will depend on the wording of the tenancy agreement. Again, if an assured tenant sublets the whole of the dwelling-house then the residence condition will no longer be satisfied. Although there is nothing to prevent the tenant resuming occupation and thus regaining the status of an assured tenant, where the tenancy is periodic the subletting of the whole will have been a breach of the tenancy agreement (see section 15 of the Housing Act 1988), and the tenant will be open to possession proceedings under ground 12 of Schedule 2 to that Act (see chapter 7).

Illegal occupation

Housing officers will be alert to the possibility that a property is being sublet, and that the tenant has left. When someone other than the tenant is in occupation the explanations following are possible:

● the occupier is a friend or relative of the tenant who is occupying the property on the tenant's behalf while the tenant is away;

● the tenant has sublet the property;

● the tenant has abandoned the property, and the occupier is a trespasser.

The first of these possibilities is quite lawful, and the tenant's security will not be lost; indeed it is being kept alive by the occupier. The tenant is under no obligation to tell the landlord about such an arrangement, although tenants should be encouraged to tell landlords when they intend to leave the property and install a friend in this way, so that confusion does not arise.

Of course, housing officers may be suspicious when an occupier explains his or her presence in this way, if the tenant has not notified his or her temporary departure. In reality the property may be being sublet, or the occupier may have gained access without the tenant's permission. Housing officers should take care to check the occupier's story. The length of the tenant's absence is a key factor in judging the occupier's version of events. If no current address for the tenant is given, then the neighbours may be able to help. Whether or not the rent is being paid should also be checked. The occupier may be asked to show evidence of the presence of the tenant's belongings on the premises; whether post is still delivered at the property for the tenant; and the names on the gas and electricity bills. An example of the kind of letter which can appropriately be sent when an illegal occupier has been discovered is set out as no 1 in the Appendix.

Abandonment and surrender

Problems may arise even when properties are found empty. The temptation is to assume that the tenant has abandoned the property, and take the opportunity to relet it. Neighbours may be able to help track down the tenant or establish when the tenant was last seen. However, as has been noted above, the tenant may still intend to return even after a prolonged absence. Of course, in most cases, personal belongings in the property will alert the housing officer to the fact that the property is still occupied, even though the tenant has not been there for some time. At the same time, it must be remembered that some tenants adopt unusual life styles, or may simply be too poor to afford many possessions. Nor should it be assumed that the tenant has abandoned the property just because items appear to be packed away in storage. The tenant may have stored their possessions in this way for safe keeping during a prolonged absence.

On the other hand, there are circumstances in which the landlord may be able to argue that the abandonment of the property amounts to a surrender of the tenancy (see chapter 12). Nevertheless, the landlord always takes a risk in treating the tenancy as having been surrendered in this way. If the tenant returns, and can demonstrate that the property was not abandoned, the tenant will be entitled to substantial damages for unlawful eviction. It is much safer for the landlord to commence possession proceedings against the tenant on the basis that security has been lost.

Example

Mr Patel owed his landlord, Southwark Borough Council, 13 months' rent. He was about to start redecorating his flat, and had removed his carpets, clothes and food, but had left some furniture. He returned home one day to find that the locks had been changed and there was a note pinned to the door instructing him to contact a named housing officer. Over the telephone the officer was abusive. The following day Mr Patel saw a different officer, who told him that the arrears were a factor in the eviction. Mr Patel paid £900 towards the arrears. The officer was unable to let Mr Patel back into the flat, as no key to the new locks could be found. On the evening of the third day Mr Patel was given a key which fitted; he had had to spend three nights sleeping on his parents' sofa. Mr Patel sued the council in Lambeth County Court and was awarded £600 general damages and £1,500 exemplary and aggravated damages (*Patel v London Borough of Southwark* September 1992 *Legal Action* 23).

Gaining possession

If the residence condition is no longer fulfilled, the tenant is no longer a secure or assured tenant, but the contractual tenancy remains unless it can be said to have been determined in another way (for example, by surrender). For the landlord to gain possession of the premises it will still be necessary to terminate the tenancy. However, once security is lost the landlord does not have to establish any ground for possession (see chapter 5). The landlord may simply serve a notice to quit in the prescribed form, and once notice has expired, the landlord may have possession (see chapter 11).

CHAPTER 5

SEEKING POSSESSION

The security provided

Common to both the Housing Act 1985 and the Housing Act 1988 is the idea that the secure or assured tenant, as long as the residence condition is satisfied, may continue to reside in the property, unless the landlord can obtain a court order against the tenant based on a specific ground stated in the statute. Certain of the grounds feature an element of fault on the part of the tenant, as where the tenant has failed to pay the rent, or is a nuisance to neighbours. Other grounds have a more managerial purpose, as where the landlord needs vacant possession of the property to carry out major repairs or improvements. Where these grounds apply, the landlord will have to provide alternative accommodation to the tenant in any event.

Grounds for seeking possession

The statutory grounds for seeking possession are considered in chapters 6 and 7. Although the court may be satisfied that as ground for posession has been made out, further conditions may also be required for a possession order to be made.

These are the bases for a possession order under the Housing Act 1985:

• any of grounds 1 to 8 is made out and it is reasonable for the court to make a possession order;

• any of grounds 9 to 11 is made out and suitable alternative accommodation is available to the tenant;

• any of grounds 12 to 16 is made out and both the reasonableness and the suitable alternative accommodation tests are met.

Under the Housing Act 1988, there are two classes of ground:

• mandatory grounds (grounds 1 to 8) if a ground is made out the court *must* make a possession order;

• discretionary grounds, (grounds 9 to 16); here a ground must be established and it must be reasonable to make the order for possession.

The factors which a court will take into account on the question of reasonableness are considered in chapter 9. Suitable alternative accommodation is dealt with in chapter 8.

Avoiding formal proceedings

Of course, if at all possible, possession proceedings should be avoided. As soon as it appears that it may be necessary to seek possession, the housing officer should write to the tenant:

• if a term of the tenancy agreement has been breached, identifying the breach, noting the term of the agreement

that has been breached, and explaining the obligation in the agreement in plain terms;
- if a managerial rather than a fault ground is relied on, explaining why possession is needed (eg what works need to be done to the premises);
- explaining the position about alternative accommodation (if appropriate);
- notifying when, where, and with whom the tenant should discuss the matter urgently, providing a name, address and telephone number;
- explaining the possibility of possession proceedings, and warning the tenant of the possible costs of those proceedings;
- emphasising that it is in the interest of both the landlord and the tenant to meet and discuss the matter amicably.

Examples of letters which may be used to try to resolve matters without possession proceedings are set out in the Appendix, items 2, 3 and 4.

Procedure

If a landlord intends to seek a court order for possession on the basis of a statutory ground, the first step is to serve a formal notice on the tenant to the effect that court proceedings will be taken.

Notice seeking possession
The notice should specify the ground, or grounds, which the landlord will be relying on and give particulars of the ground (section 83 of the Housing Act 1985; section 8 of the Housing Act 1988). This gives the tenant the opportunity to seek legal advice before proceedings take place, and even to rectify anything which he or she may have done

wrong if the ground is one which involves an element of fault on the part of the tenant. The notice need not go into lengthy detail about the grounds relied upon, but must give sufficient particulars to enable the tenant to understand the case. If possession is sought on the basis of rent arrears, the amount of the arrears must be stated. An error in the particulars given in the notice will not invalidate the notice, as long as it sets out what the landlord intends to prove in all good faith. Normally, a pre-printed standard form of notice seeking possession will be used; these forms provide spaces for the details of the particular case to be filled in. There may be insufficient space, and it is acceptable to refer to a schedule setting out the details and attach the schedule to the notice.

Examples

Torridge District Council served a notice seeking possession on Mr Jones. The only information in the notice about the reason was as follows: 'the reasons for taking this action are non-payment of rent.' This was held by the Court of Appeal to be insufficient to enable the tenant to know what he had to do to put matters right before proceedings were commenced. The amount of arrears should have been specified (*Torridge District Council v Jones* (1985) 18 HLR 107).

Dudley Metropolitan Borough Council served a notice seeking possession on Mr Bailey. The reasons for taking the action were specified as: 'Rent due to council has not been paid in that as at the 16th day of January 1989 you are in arrears to the sum of £145.96.' In fact the arrears were made up of £72.88 arrears of rent, the balance being in respect of rates and water rates. The Court of Appeal upheld the notice as valid, as it stated in summary form the facts on which the landlord intended to rely. The error in the particulars did not invalidate the notice, as the landlord had, in good faith, specified what he intended to prove at trial. The error might, however, affect the decision of the court on the merits (*Dudley Metropolitan Borough Council v Bailey* (1990) 22 HLR 424).

A landlord sought possession of premises let on an assured tenancy, under ground 8 of Schedule 1 to the Housing Act 1988 (see chapter 7). In the notice seeking possession, the ground was stated as: 'At least three months rent is unpaid.' The Court of Appeal held that this did not set out the ground for possession with sufficient detail, as it omitted to inform the tenant that there must be three months' arrears at the time of service of the notice and at the hearing, and that the rent must be lawfully due (*Mountain v Hastings* (1993) 25 HLR 427).

Notice seeking possession of a secure tenancy

A secure landlord must serve the prescribed form of notice seeking possession (section 83(2)(a) of the Housing Act 1988). The current notice is prescribed by the Secure Tenancies (Notices) Regulations 1987 (Statutory Instrument 1987 No 755), which permits forms 'substantially to the same effect' to be used. The form is set out as no 5 in the Appendix. The notice must normally specify a date after which legal proceedings may be issued (section 83(3)(a)). The date specified must not be earlier than the date when the tenancy could have been brought to an end by notice to quit. For a weekly tenancy this period will normally be four weeks (section 5 of the Protection from Eviction Act 1977). The notice remains in force for a period of one year. After that year, if the landlord still wishes to commence possession proceedings then a new notice must be served. The grounds may be altered or added to with the leave of the court (section 83(4)).

Notice seeking possession of an assured tenancy

The landlord of an assured tenant should also commence the process of seeking possession by serving a notice. It must specify the grounds on which the landlord intends to rely. The court may, however, dispense with the service of a notice if it considers it just and equitable to do so (section 8(1)(b) of the Housing Act 1988) but this possibility does not arise if the landlord wishes to rely on ground 8 (mandatory ground for possession for three months' rent arrears).

The question of when a court will feel justified in exercising its power to dispense with a notice seeking possession has not been clearly answered. Undoubtedly, if the tenant had no idea that possession proceedings were going to be commenced it would not be just and equitable to waive the requirement of notice. Conversely, if the tenant is in no way prejudiced by the lack of a notice, it would seem equitable to waive the requirement. Thus, if the tenant received a notice, but the notice did not comply with the formal requirements, or oral notice was given, with the result that the tenant was well aware of the allegations being made and that possession proceedings were envisaged, a court might be expected to exercise its discretion. Nevertheless, it is likely that a court would be willing to exercise its discretion only in favour of an individual who is a private landlord, rather than a body which provides housing, and housing officers should always ensure that a proper notice is served.

Again, the notice must be in a prescribed form (as provided by the Assured Tenancies and Agricultural Occupancies (Forms) Regulations 1988), set out as no 6 in the

Appendix. As with a notice served under the 1985 Act, particulars of the grounds relied on must be given. The grounds may later be added to or amended with the court's leave (section 8(2) of the 1988 Act). The notice must inform the tenant that court proceedings will not be commenced until after a date specified in the notice. The time which must elapse before proceedings are commenced is (section 8(3) and (4)):

- two weeks where the tenancy is for a fixed term;
- two months, whether the tenancy is for a fixed term or periodic, if the landlord is relying on grounds 1, 2, 5, 6, 7, 9 or 16;
- otherwise, if the tenancy is periodic, the earliest date when a notice to quit could have expired.

Proceedings must be commenced before the expiry of 12 months from the service of the notice seeking possession.

Fixed term tenancies: forfeiture

Although in social housing fixed term tenancies are fairly rare, both the Housing Act 1985 and the Housing Act 1988 provide for gaining possession of such tenancies. The basic security of tenure arises out of the continuation of the tenancy after the expiry of the fixed term (section 86(1) of the 1985 Act; section 5(2) of the 1988 Act).The tenancy becomes periodic and possession may be sought against the tenant as against any other periodic secure or assured tenant.

Before the expiry of the fixed term the tenancy can be brought to an end only in limited circumstances. But fixed term tenancies may be brought to an end by the landlord by forfeiture. Both the 1985 and the 1988 Acts impose restrictions on the landlord's right to forfeit the tenancy.

Forfeiture

Forfeiture, sometimes referred to as the 'right of re-entry', is a highly complicated area of the law, and is, in general, of greater importance in the context of commercial rather than residential tenancies. Forfeiture allows the landlord to treat a fixed term tenancy as at an end if the tenant has breached the terms of the tenancy agreement.

Provision for forfeiture

For the landlord to resort to forfeiture, there must be a clause in the tenancy agreement stating that forfeiture may take place. Such a clause will commonly specify that forfeiture may occur once the rent due under the tenancy has been in arrears for a specified period of time, or some other clause of the tenancy agreement is broken. The following is an example:

> If the rent hereby reserved or any part thereof shall remain unpaid for twenty one days after becoming payable (whether formally demanded or not) or if any other covenant on the part of the tenant herein contained shall not be performed or observed it shall be lawful for the landlord to re-enter upon the premises and thereupon this lease shall absolutely determine.

Notice

A landlord of residential premises can forfeit a tenancy only by way of court proceedings (section 2 of the Protection from Eviction Act 1977). Unless the landlord is relying on rent arrears as the reason for forfeiting the lease, the landlord must serve on the tenant a notice conforming to

the requirements of section 146 of the Law of Property Act 1925. The notice must:
- specify the breach of the agreement which is alleged to have taken place;
- require the breach to be remedied (if it is capable of being remedied);
- demand compensation for the breach.

Waiver

A landlord cannot rely on forfeiture if the breach of the agreement has been waived. Waiver of the breach takes place when the landlord, having become aware of the breach, does an act which is consistent only with the continuation of the tenancy. This is because, although the landlord is obliged by the Protection from Eviction Act 1977 to take possession proceedings, at common law, once the landlord has decided to forfeit the tenancy, the tenancy is at an end. It would therefore be inconsistent for the landlord to act in a way which acknowledges that a tenancy exists after stating that it is forfeit. The most common act of waiver is the demand or acceptance of rent. For example, if the landlord knows that the tenant has sublet the premises but then goes on to demand rent from the tenant, the landlord will have waived the breach of covenant in the tenancy agreement not to sublet the premises.

Relief from forfeiture

After the landlord has forfeited the tenancy the tenant is able to claim relief from forfeiture. If relief is granted then the tenancy will continue; if not, the landlord will be able to gain possession. The courts have been unwilling to lay down strict guidelines as to when the tenant will be granted this relief. In general terms, if the tenant is prepared to undertake to the court to remedy the breaches which have occurred, relief will be granted. Certain breaches, however, are considered so serious that relief may not be granted, the clearest example being breach of a covenant not to use the premises for immoral purposes.

Forfeiture actions based on rent arrears
Special rules apply to forfeiture actions in the county court based on rent arrears. The tenant is entitled to relief from forfeiture as of right if all the arrears and the costs of the action are paid into court at least five days before the date of the hearing. If this does not take place, and the arrears are proved, the landlord will be granted an order for possession, but the order must give the tenant at least four weeks to pay the arrears and the costs of the action. If this is done, relief will be granted.

Forfeiture of secure tenancies
Landlords of secure tenancies under the Housing Act 1985 (see chapter 4) may have the right to forfeit a fixed term tenancy if of course, the tenancy agreement includes a forfeiture clause. If the landlord seeks to forfeit the lease, the court is forbidden by section 82(3) of the 1985 Act from making an order for possession in pursuance of the forfeiture clause. But, if the court would otherwise have made such an order, it must make an order terminating the fixed term tenancy on a specified date. After that date the tenant will be a periodic tenant. In effect, the order reduces the length of the fixed term, and removes the added protection for the tenant that a fixed term provides. The court may choose, however, to make a possession order at the forfeiture hearing if the landlord can demonstrate that one of the grounds for possession is made out (see chapter 6).

Forfeiture of assured tenancies

A fixed term assured tenancy which contains a forfeiture clause cannot be terminated by the landlord under that clause. Accordingly, it would also seem that an assured tenant cannot claim relief from forfeiture. The landlord has to obtain an order of the court determining the tenancy, as if it was a periodic tenancy. A further limitation is that only certain grounds for possession can be relied on by an assured landlord. The court can make an order for possession only on one of the discretionary grounds in schedule 2 to the Housing Act (see chapter 7), except grounds 9 or 16 (suitable alternative accommodation available, or service tenancy). With regard to the mandatory grounds, the landlord may rely only on ground 2 (mortgagee seeking possession) or ground 8 (3 months' rent arrears). Furthermore, the forfeiture clause itself must specify that the landlord may rely on the ground in question.

CHAPTER 6

GROUNDS FOR POSSESSION AGAINST SECURE TENANTS

The grounds for possession from secure tenants are set out in Schedule 2 to the Housing Act 1985.

Grounds 1–8

If the landlord is proceeding under one or more of grounds 1 to 8, not only must the ground on grounds be made out, but, in addition, the landlord must show that it is reasonable for the court to make an order for possession. See chapter 9 for a discussion of when it is reasonable for the court to do so.

Rent arrears: ground 1

Ground 1 is that rent lawfully due from the tenant has not been paid, or another obligation of the tenancy agreement has been broken by the tenant. This is the ground most commonly used. If the landlord can demonstrate that some rent has not been paid as of the date on which proceedings are issued, then the ground is technically made out. However, the landlord must also satisfy the court that it is reasonable to make an order. The topic of rent arrears is considered further in chapter 9 in the context of reasonableness. Furthermore, rent arrears cases often result in a suspended possession order, ie, the landlord cannot actually take possession as long as the tenant continues to pay the rent, and pays a weekly or monthly sum off the rent arrears (see chapter 11).

Earlier arrears

It is rent due from the tenant against whom possession is sought which is relevant to an action under this ground. Rent arrears accrued by a former tenant or the tenant's spouse are irrelevant. This is significant if the tenant succeeded to the tenancy. The tenant will be liable only for the rent accruing after the date of succession. If a secure tenancy is transferred by way of exchange (see further C. Hunter, *Tenants' Rights*, Arden's Housing Library) the landlord may, in giving consent to the transfer, impose a condition on the tenant that any arrears of rent are paid before the tenancy is transferred (section 92(5) of the Housing Act 1985). Joint tenants are each individually liable for all the rent, and may be sued for all the rent due.

Section 48 notice

Housing officers should be aware of the Landlord and Tenant Act 1987. Section 48 of this Act requires the landlord to give the tenant, by notice, an address in England or Wales at which notices (including notices in proceedings) may be served on the landlord by the tenant. Where a landlord fails to provide such a notice any rent otherwise due from the tenant to the landlord is treated for all purposes as not being so due, until the landlord complies with the requirement. Once the landlord has served a notice, all the rent arrears which have previously accrued become due. The main intention of this provision, which applies equally to tenancies created before the 1987 Act became law, was to protect tenants whose landlords live abroad. Nonetheless, it is relevant to all residential tenancies. Local authority tenants may pay rent to one address, but deal with a different department, at another address, if their premises are in disrepair. In the absence of a clear notice as to where proceedings can be served, a tenant is able to argue that there is no cause of action at the date of the commencement of proceedings because none of the rent is due. Housing officers should ensure that a section 48 notice has been served before proceedings are commenced. Often notices of increase in rent contain the appropriate wording for the notice.

Example

In 1988 Basildon District Council had secured a suspended possession order. The tenant had since been in breach of the terms of the suspended order and the rent payment had been 'appalling.' In 1993 the tenant applied to set aside the order on the ground that none of the arrears were or had been payable because the council had never served a section 48 notice. The council conceded that notice had not been served and the district judge held that the court was 'reluctantly forced' to set aside the order. Although the council contended that its omission had been waived when the tenant later admitted the arrears, the long delay since the making of the order and/or the express waiver by the tenant's solicitors, it was held that a tenant could not waive a mandatory requirement (*Basildon District Council v Cook*, June 1994 *Legal Action* 10).

Breach of other term: ground 1

A breach of any term in the tenancy agreement may constitute a ground for possession. Normally, the tenancy agreement includes terms which in themselves give grounds for possession, eg an express obligation on the tenant not to cause nuisance or annoyance to neighbours will, if breached, be ground 1 and ground 2 (see below).

Pets

A common example of a term which does not fall under any of the specific grounds is an obligation on the tenant not to keep pets in the property. Again the court must also be satisfied as to reasonableness. The type of animal will be significant, as will the nature of the accommodation. Tenants who keep dogs in flats are a recurrent problem. On the one hand, an elderly or infirm tenant may derive comfort and security from having a dog; on the other hand, dogs are a common source of nuisance to other tenants because of noise and the fouling of common parts.

Waiver of breach

The landlord must be careful not to waive the breach. If the landlord knows that the term has, technically, been breached, but indicates to the tenant that the landlord does not mind, then the breach is said to have been waived, and the landlord will not subsequently be able to rely on that breach to seek possession.

Nuisance and annoyance: ground 2

Ground 2 falls into two parts:
● The tenant has been guilty of conduct which is a nuisance or annoyance to neighbours; or
● the tenant has been convicted of using the dwelling-

house or allowing it to be used for immoral or illegal purposes.

Definitions

'Nuisance' is an interference with the ordinary comfort of adjoining occupiers. 'Annoyance' is a wider term and includes anything which an ordinary sensible person would find a disturbance. Allowance must be made for the fact that in built up areas there must be a degree of give and take between neighbours. The nature of the locality is a factor which must be taken into account. In the words of an often quoted judicial comment, what might amount to a nuisance in Belgravia is not necessarily a nuisance in Bermondsey. Similarly, what would annoy an overly sensitive neighbour is not necessarily a nuisance or annoyance. Examples of a nuisance include noxious smells, smoke, flooding caused by overflowing baths or basins, and noise. Inherent in the concept of nuisance is a continuity of the offensive activity. Accordingly, one noisy party would not be a nuisance, but if a tenant is using the premises in a continually noisy manner then a nuisance has been created.

Visitors and those who live with the tenant

Nuisance or annoyance caused by those who visit or live with the tenant may be included as a ground for possession, but only if the tenant has failed to take all reasonable steps to prevent the nuisance. 'Neighbour' will not be construed strictly so as to mean only those who live in the buildings adjacent to the tenant's dwelling-house. If the person making the complaint against the tenant is within a reasonable distance of the tenant's home dwelling-house and so is likely to be affected by the tenant's conduct, this will suffice.

Complaints from neighbours

Complaints from neighbours may have to be viewed with caution. Sometimes neighbours may simply not get on, and housing officers may find themselves confronted with conflicting allegations from two families both alleging nuisance against the other. Landlords will not wish to be involved in domestic arguments, and in any event a court would be unlikely to make a possession order when confronted by two conflicting accounts, in the absence of evidence from people who can be said to be truly impartial. It is accordingly to be remembered that there is no obligation on a landlord to take possession proceedings under this ground (*O'Leary v London Borough of Islington* (1983) 9 HLR 81 (CA)), nor can a landlord be held liable by one tenant for the acts of nuisance of another. When confronted by such circumstances housing officers may advise the person making the complaint that it is possible for the complainant to take court proceedings for an injunction to restrain the neighbour from committing further acts of nuisance. (See further S. Belgrave, *Nuisance and Harassment*, Arden's Housing Library).

Evidence

Where a housing officer is of the opinion that a tenant is causing a nuisance regularly, and the nuisance is such that possession proceedings may have to be contemplated, even if not actually commenced, the neighbour should be asked whether or not he or she would be willing to attend court to give evidence. If not willing, the complainant should be told that without the evidence possession proceedings cannot be brought. A tenant who is willing to give evidence should be asked to keep a diary of incidents of nuisance on a set form, such as the specimen no 8 in the Appendix.

Illegal user

If a landlord is able to establish that there has been a conviction for using the property for an illegal or immoral purpose, the landlord will almost certainly succeed in obtaining a possession order, as a court will usually consider it reasonable for an order to be made in such circumstances. The classic example of immoral user is using the property as a brothel.

Connection between the offence and the premises

Illegal user will succeed only if there is some connection between the premises and the crime committed, for example, handling stolen goods on the property. If the premises were only incidental to the commission of the offence then it is unlikely that a possession order will ensue. By way of illustration, it is unlikely that an order would be made against someone convicted of possession of cannabis, who was found to have cannabis on the premises, but an order would probably be made against someone convicted of supplying cannabis from the premises.

Deterioration of premises or furniture: grounds 3 and 4

Ground 3 concerns deterioration of the premises, or the common parts; indeed, the landlord may even rely on deterioration in the state of the tenant's garden. Ground 4 covers the situation where the landlord has supplied furniture with the premises, and it has been damaged. The landlord can thus evict tenants who take no care of the property let to them. The landlord must prove that the deterioration has been caused by acts of waste, or neglect, or default on the part of the tenant or another person residing in the dwelling-house, ie, that the deterioration has not been caused by disrepair which is the landlord's responsibility.

Common Parts

Damage to common parts is included so that a tenant who keeps the flat in immaculate condition, but vandalises lifts, communal lighting or other such fixtures may be evicted under this ground.

Lodger or subtenant at fault

If the deterioration has been caused by a lodger or subtenant of the tenant, an order will not be made if the tenant has taken all reasonable steps to evict that person before the hearing.

Tenants unable to take care of their homes

Grounds 3 and 4 afford protection to the landlord against a wilfully destructive tenant. However, housing officers may encounter tenants who, through age or disability perhaps, are unable to take care of their homes in any proper fashion. A tenant who keeps a dwelling in a disgusting state may cause physical damage to property, and may well be a nuisance to adjoining occupiers, if, for instance the property is in such a filthy condition that vermin have started to appear, or smells emanate from it. Housing officers will be aware of the need to involve social services in such a case as early as possible, to help the tenant. If the property has become a health hazard the environmental health department should be asked to provide a report on the state of the property.

A court will take into account whether or not the damage caused by the tenant is wilful or a result of inadequacy when judging the question of reasonableness. If inadequacy, it is unlikely to make an order for possession unless the landlord can show that every effort has been made to help the tenant. The effect on the neighbouring tenants will be a key factor.

A vulnerable tenant may fare better in a hostel, and details of available hostel accommodation should be ascertained at the earliest opportunity.

Tenancy obtained by deception: ground 5

Ground 5, which has no equivalent under the Housing Act 1988, is that the tenant is the person, or one of the persons, to whom the tenancy was granted, and the landlord was induced to grant the tenancy by a false statement made knowingly or recklessly by the tenant. The ground involves making an allegation of fraud. Indeed, if the tenant was housed as a homeless person then a criminal offence will have been committed (section 74(1) of the Housing Act 1985). Accordingly, the burden of proof on the landlord will be high. It is the tenant who must have made the false statement. If a tenancy was granted to joint tenants, and the one who made the false statement has subsequently abandoned the property, the ground will not be available against the remaining sole tenant.

Example

Ms Watson was the secure tenant of a housing association. She was, however, dissatisfied with the property and wished to move. She applied to Rushcliffe Borough Council for housing. On the application form there was a series of boxes to tick to describe the applicant's current housing status. Rather than ticking the box for housing association tenant, Ms Watson ticked the box marked 'Sharing with family or friends.' A later application, after she had moved out of the housing association property, also failed to disclose that she had been a tenant, but stated that she had been a lodger at the property. Ms Watson was allocated a house by the council, who later discovered that she had been a tenant of the housing association.

They sought possession under ground 5, and the county court made an order accordingly. In the Court of Appeal the order was upheld, and the court stated that the judge was entitled to attach importance to the policy of discouraging deceitful applications which result in the unjust relegation on the housing list of applicants who are honest (*Rushcliffe BC v Watson* (1991) 24 HLR 124).

Exchange at a premium: ground 6

This ground is also peculiar to the Housing Act 1985. It applies if the tenancy was assigned to the tenant, or to a predecessor who is a member of the tenant's family and is living in the dwelling house. For the ground to apply, the assignment must have been made by way of exchange, and a premium must have been paid in connection with that assignment or the assignment which the tenant or predecessor made. A premium is any sum of money or other money consideration.

Employment related accommodation: ground 7

Employment-related accommodation is not necessarily excluded from the protection of the Act. Ground 7 is available to the landlord if three elements are made out:
• the dwelling-house forms part of, or is in the grounds of, a building held by the landlord for non-housing purposes;
• the letting was in consequence of employment by the landlord or a local authority, a new town corporation, a housing action trust, an urban development corporation, the Development Board for Rural Wales, or the governors of an aided school;
• the tenant or someone residing in the property has been guilty of such conduct that, having regard to the purpose

for which the building is used, it would not be right for the tenant to continue in occupation of the dwelling-house. The conduct of which the occupier is guilty must conflict in some way with the purpose for which the building is used.

Accommodation pending work: ground 8

Non-secure tenants who are moved to another property while works are being carried out to their homes do not acquire a secure tenancy of their temporary dwelling-house (paragraph 8 of Schedule 1 to the Housing Act 1985). Secure tenants, on the other hand, will be secure when moved, if the temporary accommodation becomes their only or principal home. Ground 8 allows a landlord to seek possession of the temporary accommodation. The landlord must be able to establish:

• the dwelling-house was made available for occupation by the tenant (or a predecessor) while works were carried out on the dwelling-house which the tenant previously occupied as his or her only or principal home;

• the tenant (or a predecessor) was a secure tenant of the other dwelling-house at the time of ceasing to occupy it as their home;

• the tenant (or a predecessor) accepted the tenancy of the dwelling-house of which possession is sought on the understanding that the tenant would give up occupation when, on completion of the works, the other dwelling-house was again available for occupation under a secure tenancy;

• the works have been completed and the other dwelling-house is also available.

Various factors will be relevant to the question of reasonableness: the reasons for undertaking the works; how long the tenant had occupied the former home; how long the works took to be completed; how long the tenant was told the works would take.

Grounds 9–11

If the landlord relies on one or more of grounds 9 to 11, it must be shown that the ground is made out, and that suitable alternative accommodation is available to the tenant. Suitable alternative accommodation is considered in chapter 8.

Overcrowding: ground 9

Ground 9, which has no equivalent in the Housing Act 1988, is made out where the dwelling-house is overcrowded within the meaning of Part XI of the Housing Act 1985, in such circumstances as to render the occupier guilty of an offence.

There are two tests for overcrowding: the room standard and the space standard. If either test is failed then the premises are overcrowded. There are also several defences, such as natural growth, which mean that even although the dwelling-house is overcrowded the occupier is not committing an offence. In relation to possession proceedings under this ground, rather surprisingly, alternative accommodation will not be deemed unsuitable even if it offends the space standard.

Landlord's works: grounds 10 and 10A

Ground 10 enables the landlord to obtain possession if it

can be established that the landlord intends, within a reasonable time of seeking possession, to do one of the following:

● demolish or reconstruct the building, or part of the building which includes the dwelling-house;

● carry out work on the building, or on land let together with the building.

In either case, the landlord must also be able to demonstrate that the works cannot reasonably be done without obtaining possession. This is a question on which the surveyor in charge of the works should be asked to comment.

Ground 10A was introduced to address the situation where redevelopment is intended, but the landlord will not be carrying out the works. The landlord must establish:

● an intention to sell the premises with vacant possession within a reasonable time of obtaining possession;

● that the property, or part of it, is in an approved development area (ie, approved by the Secretary of State or, in the case of a registered housing association, the Housing Corporation).

Charitable purposes: ground 11

This ground applies only where the landlord is a charity within the meaning of the Charities Act 1993. The landlord must prove that the tenant's continued occupation of the dwelling-house conflicts with the purposes of the charity, eg the charity provides accommodation for disabled people, and neither the tenant nor anyone now living with the tenant is disabled.

Ground 12–16

A landlord relying on one or more of grounds 12 to 16 must

demonstrate that the ground is made out, *and* that suitable alternative accommodation is available for the tenant; *and* that it is reasonable to make an order for possession. Suitable alternative accommodation is considered in chapter 8. Reasonableness is dealt with in chapter 9.

Non-housing property required for employee: ground 12

Ground 12 applies when the landlord can show that the property:

- forms part of, or is in the grounds of, a non-housing building, or in the grounds of a cemetery;
- was let to the tenant in consequence of employment;
- is now reasonably required for a new employee.

Accommodation for the disabled: ground 13

Ground 13 applies if the dwelling-house has features which are substantially different from those of ordinary dwelling-houses, and which are designed to make the dwelling suitable for occupation by a physically disabled person who requires accommodation of a kind provided by the dwelling-house. The landlord must establish that:

- there is no longer such a person residing in the dwelling-house;
- the landlord requires it for occupation (whether alone or with members of his or her family) by such a person.

Special needs accommodation: ground 14

Ground 14 is available only to landlords who are housing associations or housing trusts, who let dwelling-houses for occupation only by persons whose circumstances (other than financial circumstances) make it especially difficult for them to satisfy their housing needs. The landlord has to establish one of the following:

- there is no longer such a person residing in the dwelling-house;
- the tenant has received from a local housing authority an offer of accommodation in premises which are to be let as a separate dwelling under a secure tenancy.

Furthermore, it must be proved that:

- the landlord requires the dwelling-house for occupation (whether alone or with members of his or her family) by such a person.

Sheltered accommodation: ground 15

Ground 15 applies to 'sheltered accommodation'. The dwelling-house must be part of a group of flats or houses which are let to people with special needs, and which are in close proximity to a social service or special facility. Housing provided for the disabled or the elderly are common examples. As under grounds 13 and 14, the ground is established only if there is no longer a person of the designated class in occupation, and the dwelling-house is required for such a person.

Under-occupation: ground 16

Ground 16 is available only where the tenant has succeeded to the secure tenancy on the death of the previous tenant. It is not available where there has been an assignment to someone entitled to succeed. Nor is it available when the tenant is the spouse of the deceased former tenant. The landlord may rely on this ground only if:

- the dwelling is more extensive than is reasonably required by the successor;

● a notice of seeking possession was served no earlier than six months after the death of the previous tenant, and no later that 12 months after the death.

CHAPTER 7

GROUNDS FOR POSSESSION AGAINST ASSURED TENANTS

The grounds for possession against assured tenants are set out in Schedule 2 to the Housing Act 1988. Many of the grounds are not of interest to housing officers and managers, having been designed essentially for the private sector rather than for social landlords, and they are not considered at length here. Most such grounds are among the mandatory grounds. By way of example, ground 1 concerns home owners who let their homes. If the owner gives the correct notice to the tenant before the beginning of the tenancy, there is a mandatory ground for possession.

It will also be noted that many of the grounds are similar to those included in the Housing Act of 1985, discussed in chapter 6.

Grounds 1–8 are mandatory. If the landlord can establish as a matter of fact that the ground is made out, then a possession order *must* be made. Grounds 9–16 are discretionary, and in these cases the landlord must also establish that it is reasonable for a possession order to be made.

Mandatory grounds

Returning home owner: ground 1

This ground applies to a home owner who has served a notice on the tenant before the commencement of the tenancy telling the tenant that possession may later be required under this ground. The landlord has to establish either that he or she used to occupy the property as his or her only or principal home, or that the landlord or the landlord's spouse intends to occupy it as such.

Mortgaged property: ground 2

This ground is available when the property is mortgaged, and the mortgage predates the grant of the tenancy. It applies if the mortgagee is entitled to exercise the power of sale and requires possession to sell the property. Notice under ground 1 must have been served by the landlord.

Holiday letting out of season: ground 3

Student letting: ground 4

Ministers of religion: ground 5

Landlord's works: ground 6

This ground is similar to ground 10 under the 1985 Act. It enables the landlord to obtain vacant possession to carry out works to the premises. The landlord must intend to demolish or reconstruct the whole or a substantial part of the premises, or carry out substantial works on them. The ground does not apply if intended work could reasonably be carried out without the tenant giving up possession of the dwelling-house. But it will apply if the work cannot be carried out without the tenant's vacating the dwelling for one of the following reasons:

• the tenant is unwilling to agree to such a variation of the terms of the tenancy as would give such access and other facilities as would permit the intended work to be carried out;

• the nature of the intended work is such that no such variation is practicable;

• the tenant is not willing to accept an assured tenancy of such part only of the dwelling-house as would leave in the possession of the landlord so much of the dwelling-house as would be reasonable to enable the intended work to be carried out and, where appropriate, as would give such access and other facilities over the reduced part as would permit the intended work to be carried out;

• the nature of the intended work is such that such a tenancy is not practicable.

The ground is also available to a registered housing association or a charitable housing trust, where the person intending to do the works is not the landlord, but a superior landlord. The ground is not available to a landlord who has bought the property for money, or money's worth, with the tenant in occupation.

Inherited tenancy: ground 7

This ground is available only where the tenant is a periodic tenant. It applies when the tenancy has passed under the will of a tenant, or on the tenant's intestacy, but not when it has devolved by statutory succession. (See C. Hunter, *Tenants' Rights*, Arden's Housing Library, for details of where there is an entitlement to a statutory succession.) Proceedings must be commenced within one year of the tenant's death, or, if the court so allows, one year after the landlord became aware of the death of the tenant. The ground specifies that if the landlord continues to accept rent from the successor, this will not amount to the creation of a new tenancy, unless the landlord has agreed in writing to a change in the terms of the tenancy, including the amount of rent, or the period of the tenancy, or the extent of the property let.

Rent arrears: ground 8

The Housing Act 1985 provides only one ground relating to rent arrears (ground 1). The 1988 Act prescribes three grounds (see also grounds 10 and 11). Landlords under the 1988 Act have the advantage of a mandatory ground for possession for rent arrears. Ground 8 is available if, both at the date of service of the notice seeking possession and at the date of hearing the action, an amount of rent, calculated as set out below, is outstanding:

- if rent is payable weekly or fortnightly, at least 13 weeks' rent;
- if rent is payable monthly, at least three months' rent;
- if rent is payable quarterly, at least one quarter's rent is more than three months in arrears;
- if rent is payable yearly, at least three months' rent is more than three months in arrears.

Discretionary grounds

In all the following cases the court must be satisfied both that the ground for possession is made out, and that it is reasonable to make an order for possession. Reasonableness is considered further in chapter 9.

Suitable alternative accommodation: ground 9

It will have been noted that Schedule 2 to the Housing Act 1988 does not include grounds where suitable alternative accommodation has to be provided in addition to making out other requirements. This is because suitable alternative accommodation is in itself a ground for possession. What constitutes suitable alternative accommodation is considered further in chapter 8.

Rent arrears: grounds 10 and 11

Grounds 10 and 11 both provide grounds for possession in relation to rent arrears (see also ground 8 above). Ground 10 applies where some rent lawfully due from the tenant:
- is unpaid on the date on which the proceedings for possession are begun; and
- except where the court finds it is just and equitable to dispense with the service of a notice seeking possession (section 8(1)(b) of the Housing Act 1988), was in arrears at the date of service of the notice seeking possession.

Ground 11 is available whether or not any rent is in arrears on the date possession proceedings are begun. The landlord must establish that the tenant has persistently delayed paying rent which has become lawfully due. This ground provides a remedy against tenants who delay paying the rent until the last possible moment before possession proceedings are begun.

Breach of term of tenancy: ground 12

Ground 12 concerns the breach of any term of the tenancy, save the payment of rent. See ground 1 under the 1985 Act, chapter 6.

Deterioration of dwelling-house: ground 13
See ground 3 under the 1985 Act, chapter 6.

Nuisance and annoyance: ground 14
See ground 2 under the Housing Act 1985, chapter 6. This ground differs, however, in that the words 'adjoining occupiers' are used instead of 'neighbours'. The courts have held that there is no material difference between the two phrases.

Deterioration of furniture: ground 15
See ground 4 under the Housing Act 1985, chapter 6.

Tied accommodation: ground 16
Ground 16 relates to accommodation let to employees. The landlord must show that:
- the dwelling-house was let to the tenant in consequence of the tenant's employment by the landlord seeking possession or by a previous landlord under the tenancy;
- the tenant has ceased to be in that employment.

CHAPTER 8

SUITABLE ALTERNATIVE ACCOMMODATION

When a possession order is sought pursuant to any of grounds 9 to 16 under the Housing Act 1985, the court must be satisfied that suitable alternative accommodation is available. In addition, the availability of suitable alternative accommodation is in itself a ground for possession under the Housing Act 1988 (ground 9). Part IV of Schedule 2 to the 1985 Act sets out certain requirements concerning the suitability of the alternative accommodation. A similar list of requirements appears in Part III of Schedule 2 to the 1988 Act.

Secure tenants

Alternative accommodation will be considered suitable only if the tenant will have security of tenure similar to that already enjoyed. Accordingly, the accommodation will be suitable only if it is to be let under a secure tenancy, an assured tenancy, or a protected tenancy under the Rent Act 1977. A shorthold tenancy (see chapter 10) will not suffice, nor will a tenancy granted under the Housing Act 1988 which is subject to mandatory grounds for possession (eg the owner of the property intends to return to it at some stage and gives the tenant notice to this effect).

Needs of the tenant

The accommodation must be reasonably suitable to the needs of the tenant and the tenant's family. In determining this question, the following factors must be considered:

● the nature of the accommodation which it is the practice of the landlord to allocate to persons with similar needs (eg the council will probably allocate properties according to the size of the tenant's family);

● the distance of the accommodation from the place of work or education of the tenant and the members of the family. A tenant cannot be expected to have to spend substantially longer travelling to work each day, nor should it be more difficult for the tenant's children to get to school each morning;

● distance from the home of any member of the tenant's family if proximity to it is essential to that person's, or the tenant's, well-being;

● the terms on which the accommodation is available and the terms of the secure tenancy;

● if furniture was provided by the landlord for use under the secure tenancy, whether furniture is to be provided in the other accommodation, and the nature of that furniture.

This list is not exhaustive, and the tenant may introduce other matters to be taken into account. The weight to be accorded to each factor will be a matter of fact and degree in each case. The needs of a tenant's family may include the need for a garden if the tenant's hobbies include gardening. Regard must be had to the needs of the tenant's family as well as those of the tenant, even where a husband and wife have separated. Indeed, other members of the family are entitled to take part in the proceedings and to be heard on this issue (*London Borough of Wandsworth v Fadayomi* (1987) 19 HLR 512 CA)).

Allocation policy

In practice, when the landlord is a local authority the most significant factor is likely to be the nature of the accommodation which the authority allocates to persons with similar needs. The inclusion of this matter for consideration acknowledges that local authorities do not have unlimited resources and allows the court to take into account the needs of other homeless persons in the area. Effectively, the court is being asked to take into account a local housing authority's duty pursuant to section 22 of the Housing Act 1985, under which the authority is bound to give a reasonable preference, in allocating of housing, to people occupying overcrowded or insanitary dwellings; or who have large families; or who are living in unsatisfactory conditions; or who are homeless.

Despite the fact that most people are aware of the pressures on the public sector, many judges are still surprised when presented with the figures. Statistics should be submitted in evidence to demonstrate the authority's policy, and the reason a dwelling of a particular size and character is considered suitable should be clearly stated in the context of the policy.

Example

Mr French was a secure tenant of Enfield Borough Council. He had succeeded to the tenancy as the son of the former tenant. The council sought possession on the basis that the property was too big for his reasonable requirements (Housing Act 1985, ground 16). The property was a two bedroomed flat with a garden. A number of offers of alternative accommodation were made, the last of which was a one bedroomed flat, without a garden, in a less pleasant area. Mr French did not consider the flat suitable. He contended that he required a second bedroom to accommodate his brother, who was a frequent visitor, the area was worse, and he needed a garden. Evidence was given that he had created a beautiful garden. Nevertheless the judge made an order for possession. Mr French unsuccessfully appealed to the Court of Appeal, where it was held that a garden can qualify as one of a tenant's needs, but an offer of alternative accommodation may still be suitable even if one of the tenant's needs is not met. The visiting brother could easily have been accommodated in the living room. Evidence had been given of the demand for council housing in the area, and the policy which had been developed by Enfield Borough Council to cope with this demand. This evidence was the decisive factor in the case (*Enfield London Borough Council v French* (1984) 17 HLR 211).

Local authority certificate

Where the landlord is not a local authority, a certificate from the local authority that suitable alternative accommodation will be provided by that authority will be conclusive evidence that alternative accommodation so provided is suitable.

Assured tenants

Ground 9 under the 1988 Act applies where suitable alternative accommodation is available or will be available for the tenant when the possession order takes effect.

Local authority certificate

The landlord may be able to rely on a certificate from a local authority stating that the tenant will be rehoused by the authority. Such a certificate is conclusive evidence that suitable alternative accommodation will be available to the tenant by the date specified in the certificate.

If the landlord is not relying on such a certificate, the landlord will have to provide the tenant with a tenancy of another property owned by the landlord, or ensure that another landlord makes a property available.

Suitability

The new tenancy must give the tenant similar security of tenure; it cannot be an assured shorthold (see chapter 10), or an assured tenancy to which one of the mandatory grounds 1 to 5 under the Housing Act 1988 will apply. The tenancy need not be assured.

Part III of Schedule 2 to the 1988 Act requires that the alternative accommodation is:

• reasonably suitable to the needs of the tenant and their family as regards proximity to place of work; and either

• similar, in terms of rental and extent, to the accommodation afforded by such a dwelling-house as would be provided in the neighbourhood by any local housing authority, for persons whose needs as regards extent are, in the opinion of the court, similar to those of the tenant and their family; or

• reasonably suitable to the means of the tenant and to the

needs of the tenant and their family as regards extent and character.

Furniture

Furthermore, if the tenant had formerly been provided with furniture there must be furniture in the alternative accommodation which is either similar to that formerly provided or reasonably suitable to the needs of the tenant and their family.

Comparison with local authority practice

The comparison with what the tenant could expect from a local authority is to be noted. The extent of accommodation provided by the local authority is proved by a certificate from the authority, but the judge must still consider whether or not the proposed alternative accommodation is similar to it.

Reluctant tenants

The most common complaint of tenants is that the proposed alternative is simply not as good as the current home. The courts emphasise that the purpose behind the Act is to provide people with homes, not to meet the individual tastes and preferences of particular tenants. A difference in the character of the two properties will render an offer unsuitable only if the difference is one of kind rather than degree.

It is to be remembered that the ground is discretionary, and so the judge must also consider whether it is reasonable to make an order for possession. Often the tenant will seek to argue that, although the accommodation is suitable by reference to the criteria in the schedule, it is not reasonable to make an order because the alternative accommodation is far below the standard of the current home. Such an argument should rarely succeed, as it is in effect an attempt to reopen the question of suitability.

Location

The location of the proposed property in relation to the tenant's place of work is a factor specified in the schedule. It is not, though, possible to take into account the fact that the tenant may have to move away from friends or cultural and religious centre. See *Siddiqui v Rashid* [1980] 1 WLR 1018, which concerned a muslim tenant who would not be able to attend his mosque if he had to move to the proposed alternative accommodation.

CHAPTER 9

REASONABLENESS

If the landlord is proceeding under grounds 1 to 8, or 12 to 16 of the 1985 Act, or under grounds 9 to 16 of the 1988 Act, the landlord must demonstrate that it is reasonable for an order for possession to be made. The requirement of reasonableness is additional to the requirements in the grounds themselves, and to the requirement for suitable alternative accommodation in the case of grounds 12 to 16 of the 1985 Act. However, it would be unusual for the test of reasonableness not to be satisfied if it has been demonstrated that suitable alternative accommodation is available, unless the tenant is very elderly or infirm, in which case moving the tenant may be unreasonable.

Judge's discretion

When the case is based on a discretionary ground, the judge must make a finding on the question of reasonableness or the judgment will be open to appeal and the case will have to be re-tried. The question of reasonableness is one of fact and degree in each case, and is a matter for the judge to decide. The decision will rarely be open to appeal, unless the judge has obviously taken into account a completely irrelevant factor, or has exercised judgment in an irrational way.

Circumstances to be considered

In considering reasonableness, the judge is entitled to take into account all relevant circumstances as they exist at the date of the hearing. Particular factors which bear on the question of reasonableness (and the weight to be accorded to them) vary according to the ground for possession being relied upon. The issue of reasonableness involves balancing the hardship to the tenant if the possession order is made, and the hardship to the landlord if it is not. An elderly tenant who has lived in one place for many years is clearly in a stronger position than a young tenant in employment who has lived in a property for a short time.

Interests of the tenant
The personal circumstances of the tenant, and of those who live with the tenant are plainly relevant. These will include:
- the age of the tenant;
- whether or not the tenant is employed;
- whether or not the tenant has children;
- the health of the tenant and the family;
- the length of the tenant's occupation of the property.

Interests of the landlord
The tenant's circumstances are balanced against the reasons the landlord is seeking possession. Social landlords

are in a different position from commercial landlords and small landlords to whom the income from a property may be vital. Social landlords are not seeking to make a profit, but to satisfy the public interest in the provision of housing. This cuts both ways. On the one hand, an individual who lets a house as his or her only source of income will suffer greatly if the payment of rent is delayed. Public authorities and housing associations have come to be expected to be able to tolerate higher levels of arrears. On the other hand they are not motivated by commercial objectives, but rather by considerations for their other tenants and those who may be awaiting housing. Accordingly, they are often in a better position to argue that it is reasonable to grant possession than are landlords whose concerns are purely commercial. Furthermore, local authorities may also now point to the effects of the Local Government and Housing Act 1989. The court may be referred to the requirement imposed on local authorities to balance their Housing Revenue Account. It may be argued with some force that tenants' arrears may lead to an increase in rent for others, and the local authority must have regard to the welfare of all tenants.

Nuisance cases

Similar considerations apply to proceedings brought on the ground of nuisance. Social landlords are expected to provide housing for those who may find it difficult to look after themselves, particularly in the light of the current policy of 'care in the community'. Sometimes such tenants may be a nuisance to their neighbours, because of noise, occasional strange behaviour, or lack of cleanliness. In considering the question of reasonableness, a judge is bound to take note that, if evicted, someone of this type will have no hope of obtaining housing elsewhere. Proceedings for eviction should thus be used only if absolutely necessary.

Social services must always be contacted, as they may be able to help stop the nuisance, and this will show that the landlord has acted reasonably. A social worker may be able to give evidence to the court that the tenant needs help and would be better served by being accommodated in a hostel.

Rent arrears

In rent arrears cases, the amount of the arrears will obviously be an important factor in deciding resonableness.

Amount

Many tenants receive housing benefit, and have to pay only a 'top up' which may be a relatively small sum. Some judges do not consider it reasonable to make an order for possession if less than a certain amount of money is owing. There is no reason why this should be so. A relatively small figure, say £200, may represent months of rent arrears if the tenant is obliged to pay only a top up of £2.20 a week. It is always vital that the housing officer is in a position to demonstrate persistent failure to pay rent, and the efforts made by the landlord, such as letters to the tenant explaining the situation, or visits by the housing officer to discuss the matter. A tenant who has made no effort to communicate with the landlord about the arrears is open to criticism. Informal arrangements to pay off the arrears at a particular rate may have been made. If the tenant has failed to make the payments under such an arrangement the landlord's case will be strengthened.

Effect of notice seeking possession

Of particular importance is the way in which the tenant reacts to the notice seeking possession. A tenant who, in response, pays a lump sum off the arrears, and then pays the rent when it becomes due, is in a much stronger position than one who continues to default.

Reasons for arrears

In some cases, a change in the tenant's circumstances causes arrears to accrue. Illness or loss of employment, coupled with delay in the processing of a claim for housing benefit, may be the reason. Or a tenant may have been bereaved and has had to pay for the funeral.

Possession proceedings based on rent arrears must now be brought on a particular court form, form N119. Significantly the form includes paragraphs concerning the landlord's previous efforts to recover the arrears, and the details known to the landlord of the tenant's financial circumstances. These factors both go to reasonableness and housing officers must ensure that they are in a position to fill in these paragraphs with full details.

Counterclaims for disrepair

Often, the arrears have accrued because the tenant has deliberately withheld rent, alleging that the landlord has failed to comply with the landlord's obligations to keep the property in repair. A tenant should in fact continue to pay the rent regardless of any breach by the landlord of the repairing covenant. But the tenant will be able to counterclaim for damages for non-repair at the trial. If the tenant is successful, the amount of damages will be set off against the amount of rent owed to the landlord. The arrears may be extinguished or dramatically reduced, and a possession order will not be made. Recent awards of damages for disrepair indicated that substantial amounts are possible.

If, though, the counterclaim is unsuccessful, then it will

not normally be reasonable to make an order for posses-sion without giving the tenant the opportunity to pay off the arrears. A tenant who has been well advised will have continued to pay the rent into a special bank or building society account, and so will be in a position to pay the arrears. If the tenant cannot clear the arrears within a rea-sonable period of time, a possession order will be made. In fact, a court is likely to make a suspended possession order on condition that the tenant pay the arrears within a spec-ified time (see chapter 11).

Rent and housing benefit

The tenant may be contractually obliged to pay rent in advance, ie at the beginning of the period of the tenancy, but housing benefit may be paid in arrears, ie, at the end of the period, or even in lump sums when substantial arrears have accrued. In such circumstances it will not be reasonable to make a possession order under ground 11 of the 1988 Act (persistent delay in paying rent) as the preju-dice to the landlord is minimal, and the default in the pay-ment of rent is not within the tenant's control.

Suspended orders

It should always be remembered that outright possession orders are rare in rent arrears cases. It is more usual for a suspended order to be made (see chapter 11).

Example

Mr and Mrs Taylor were secure tenants of the house where they had lived for 24 years. Mr Taylor had become unemployed, and was having tax problems. Mrs Taylor had diabetes and was attending a specialist for treat-ment. They were in considerable arrears of rent, were

> receiving housing benefit by the time of the trial. The registrar considered it reasonable to make an order for possession. On appeal to a judge a new trial was ordered. The council appealed to the Court of Appeal against the ruling of the judge. The Court of Appeal dismissed the council's appeal. It was said that there was 'difficulty in understanding how anyone could have made an order turning them out of their home' (*Woodspring District Council v Taylor* (1982) 4 HLR 95).

Breach of other term

In cases founded on breach of an obligation of the tenancy, other than to pay rent, much will turn on the seriousness of the breach, and the intention of the tenant. A trivial breach which cannot affect the landlord will not justify a possession order.

Remedying the breach

The tenant's reactions to the landlord's request to remedy the breach are of great importance. A tenant may have breached the tenancy agreement in all innocence, having failed to realise that what was being done was a breach. If, on being given notice of the breach the tenant takes action to remedy it, it will not normally be reasonable to make the order. Similarly, if the tenant has been causing a nuisance or annoyance to neighbours, but has abated the nuisance by the time of the possession hearing, it would be unusual for a court to consider it reasonable to make an order. Nevertheless, if there has been a long history of nuisance, or the acts of annoyance were very disturbing, then a possession order may still be made. This might be the case if the tenant has been guilty of racial harassment on an estate.

In general terms the tenant should be allowed the opportunity to rectify matters. If the state of the premises has deteriorated, the tenant should be given enough time to carry out the repairs, or to reimburse the landlord for the cost of repairs. Breach of the term not to use the premises for immoral purposes, however, is viewed as incapable of remedy, and so, although the immoral use may have ceased, it will be reasonable to make a possession order in these circumstances.

If the tenant proposes to continue the activity which breached the tenancy agreement, then the landlord is likely to succeed on the question of reasonableness.

Example

> Mrs Jepson was the secure tenant of a flat. It was a term of her tenancy that she could not keep a dog in the flat, which shared common parts and common means of access with other flats in the block. Despite being requested by her landlord to remove the dog, Mrs Jepson refused to do so, saying she kept the dog for her personal protection, and that of her young child. Evidence was given of complaints to the caretaker of the block about nuisance caused by dogs. The judge held that it was not reasonable to make an order for possession. The Court of Appeal allowed an appeal by the landlord. The breach had deliberately been continued by the tenant, and there was evidence that dogs adversely affected the enjoyment of the estate by the other tenants (*Sheffield City Council v Jepson* (1993) 25 HLR 299 CA).

Council policy

The courts have held that the impropriety or otherwise of a council's policy is not a factor relevant to the judge's exercise of discretion regarding reasonableness. The judge should be concerned with the reasonableness in the particular case of ordering possession. Effectively, the court is not able to review council policy when deciding the question of reasonableness.

Example

> Mr and Mrs Hyatt were secure tenants of a house. Mr Hyatt was unemployed, and Mrs Hyatt was severely disabled. Their tenancy agreement provided: 'the tenant shall not, except with the permission of the council, park any caravan in the front or back garden of the dwelling'. Mr and Mrs Hyatt kept a caravan in their front garden. Having the caravan allowed them to go on holiday despite Mrs Hyatt's disability. There were no alternative sites in the area, although the caravan could be parked some distance away at a cost of £200 per year. The Hyatt's asked the council's permission to keep the caravan in the garden. The council refused, since as a matter of housing policy permission was never granted. The council requested that the caravan be removed. Mr and Mrs Hyatt unsuccessfully appealed to a housing sub-committee. The council sought possession under ground 1 (breach of term of tenancy agreement). The judge found it was not reasonable to order possession, because of the council's policy of never giving permission to site a caravan regardless of personal circumstances. The council successfully appealed against this decision. It was held that the judge should not be concerned with the propriety of a policy rule, but should consider only the reasonableness of the particular case. A new trial was ordered (*London Borough of Barking and Dagenham v Hyatt and Hyatt* (1991) 24 HLR 406).

CHAPTER 10

OTHER OCCUPIERS

In this chapter types of occupier who have only limited security of tenure are considered. In such cases, it is not necessary for the landlord to demonstrate that there is a ground for possession. As long as the landlord conforms to the correct procedure for giving notice to the tenant that possession is required the tenant will have to give possession to the landlord.

Assured shorthold

An assured shorthold tenancy is a type of assured tenancy under the Housing Act 1988. Accordingly, it can be granted only by a landlord capable of granting an assured tenancy, not by any of the landlords who grant secure tenancies, see chapter 3.

Purposes

The idea of an assured shorthold tenancy is to provide a fixed term letting, at the end of which the landlord is able to recover possession without having to prove grounds. Assured shorthold was introduced mainly to encourage private landlords who might want to let properties for a short time only, or who were concerned about being unable to remove bad tenants. In particular, shorthold is ideal for a home owner who wishes to let the home while working abroad for a time.

Nevertheless, assured shortholds are of interest not only to private landlords. Housing associations may find assured shortholds a suitable way of letting to those who have an immediate and temporary need for accommodation.

Features

An assured shorthold tenancy must be a fixed term tenancy. The term must be at least six months. The landlord must serve a notice on the tenant before the tenancy is entered into stating that the tenancy is an assured shorthold tenancy (section 20 of the Housing Act 1988). If the landlord fails to serve this notice, at the expiry of the fixed term the tenant will be a fully assured periodic tenant. The notice must give the correct details of the agreement, so that where a notice stated a period of six months, but the tenancy was in fact for 12 months, the notice was held to be invalid (*Panayi v Roberts* (1993) 25 HLR 408 (CA)).

A tenancy will not be an assured shorthold tenancy if immediately beforehand, the person to whom the tenancy was granted (or if it is granted to joint tenants, one of them) was an assured tenant under the Housing Act 1988. This prevents landlords persuading tenants to accept tenancies with less security than they already have.

Possession

During the term of the tenancy the landlord is able to gain possession only if he can forfeit the lease (see chapter 5). Once the term has expired the tenant will become a periodic tenant, but the landlord has an absolute right to possession if the tenant is served with the correct notice. There are two different notices.

- The landlord may serve a notice under section 21(1)(b) of the 1988 Act before the end of the fixed term. It has simply to give two months' notice.
- If the landlord fails to serve a notice before the end of the fixed term, the landlord will have to serve a notice under section 21(4) of the Act. Such a notice must, again, give two months notice, but must also specify a date which is the last day of a period of the tenancy, but not earlier than the last day on which the tenancy could be brought to an end by notice to quit. Finally, the notice must also state that possession is required by virtue of section 21(4) of the Housing Act 1988.

New shorthold

If the landlord wants to grant the tenant a new assured shorthold tenancy after the expiry of the term that may be done. No new notice is required before entering into this new contract, for the tenancy is deemed to be an assured shorthold (section 20(4) of the Housing Act 1988). The landlord may instead choose to grant a full assured tenancy, if that is thought appropriate, by serving a notice to that effect on the tenant (section 20(5)).

Accelerated procedure in the county court

There is a swift means of obtaining possession of premises let under an assured shorthold tenancy under rules 6 and 6A of order 49 of the County Court Rules. However, this procedure is available to the landlord only if possession alone is sought. If the landlord also wishes to recover rent arrears, or damages for deterioration of the dwelling, then this accelerated procedure is not available.

Protection from eviction

Housing officers will encounter occupiers who have no security under either the Housing Act 1985 or the Housing Act 1988. It must be remembered that all tenants, and most licensees, are entitled to remain in occupation until a possession order is made (Protection from Eviction Act 1977). Indeed, it is a criminal offence to evict such an occupier without first obtaining a court order.

Notice to quit

The process for obtaining possession where there is no security of tenure is commenced by serving a notice to quit the premises, ie a notice stating when the tenant must deliver up possession to the landlord. Under the Protection from Eviction Act 1977 a notice to quit must be in writing and contain prescribed information. The purpose of the prescribed information is to enable the tenant to realise the seriousness of the proceedings, and to alert him or her to the possibility of obtaining advice on the feasibility of defending the case. Notices seeking possession under the Housing Acts of 1985 and 1988 must contain similar paragraphs. To avoid the possibility of error, it is always advisable to use a standard form notice to quit. An example appears as no 7 in the Appendix to this book.

Period of notice

The period of notice required may be specified in the tenancy agreement. Under section 5(1)(a) of the Protection from Eviction Act 1977 there is a minimum period of notice of four weeks. The notice period is calculated by reference to the period of the tenancy, ie the intervals at which the rent is paid. Accordingly, if the tenancy is a monthly tenancy a month's notice will be required, if the tenancy is quarterly a notice of one quarter will be required. Most of the tenancies encountered in the social housing sector are weekly tenancies, which require a notice period of four weeks. Monthly tenancies are almost always tenancies by reference to calendar, not lunar, months, and a notice to quit served on a monthly periodic tenant giving four weeks notice to quit would be invalid.

In addition the notice period must expire on a day which is the last day of a period of the tenancy. If, for example, the tenancy is weekly and rent is paid on Fridays, then the last day of any period is the Thursday. Computing the day on which the period expires can be complicated. Any error in the wording of the notice to quit, save obvious and minor clerical errors, will invalidate the notice and any proceedings based on it. All standard notices to quit accordingly use the form:

> 'I hereby give you notice to quit on the . . . day of . . . 19 . . or at the expiration of the period of your tenancy which shall expire next after the expiration of four weeks from the service upon you of this notice'.

This has been held to be a permissible way of avoiding the problems which may arise from an error in the date given in the notice.

Service

If the notice is in the correct form, and properly served on the tenant, then a tenant, who cannot claim to have any security of tenure will have no defence to the possession action. Proof of service of the notice to quit is vital. The notice to quit may be served personally on the tenant by an officer delivering it or service may be effected by post. The notice is not validly served until the tenant himself or herself receives it, although it may be left with someone, such as a spouse, who may be treated as acting as the tenant's agent. If the tenancy is held by joint tenants, and only one lives in the premises, it is sufficient to serve the notice on that tenant, but the notice should be addressed to all the joint tenants.

The landlord may find that the tenant no longer lives in the premises. If the tenancy agreement was in writing this should not present a problem. The notice to quit is sufficiently served if it is sent by registered post or recorded delivery addressed to the tenant by name at the tenant's last known place of residence or business in the United Kingdom (section 196 of the Law of Property Act 1925 and section 1 of the Recorded Delivery Act 1962). If the letter is not returned by the Post Office undelivered, service is deemed to have taken place at the time at which the letter would in the ordinary course of the postal system be delivered. The landlord needs to demonstrate to the court that the letter was prepaid, properly addressed and posted. It is also sufficient service if the landlord leaves the notice at the tenant's last known residential or business address in the United Kingdom.

Abandoned premises

The most common situation in which possession will be

regained by the simple service of a notice to quit is where the tenant has abandoned the premises, and they are either empty, or occupied by someone who has no agreement with the landlord. The tenant fails to satisfy the residence condition (see chapter 4), and can be neither secure nor assured. Anyone in occupation is there without the permission of the landlord and is accordingly a trespasser. Although the security of tenure is lost, the tenant still has a contract with the landlord which must be determined by service of notice to quit.

Other occasions when service of a notice to quit will be required derive from the exceptions to the creation of assured or secure tenancies set out in Schedule 1 to both the 1985 Act and the 1988 Act. Common examples are:

- short life user lettings;
- lettings to homeless persons before twelve months have elapsed;
- lettings under subleasing schemes.

In addition, landlords who are subject neither to the Housing Act 1985 nor to the Housing Act 1988 (eg government departments who let property) will terminate tenancy agreements in this way.

Matrimonial homes

It has already been emphasised that security of tenure is afforded to the tenant, and the tenant alone.

Cohabitees

Those who live with the tenant are, at common law, only the tenant's licensees and have no rights against the landlord. Accordingly, it is desirable for cohabitees to be named as joint tenants in the tenancy agreement. (For the break-up of a relationship between joint tenants see chapter 12).

Spouses

At common law, spouses who were not joint tenants, but had domestic disputes, or whose relationships broke up, were in a vulnerable position. The Matrimonial Homes Act 1983, however, now provides additional rights for spouses against each other and their landlords.

Right to remain in the matrimonial home

One party to a marriage cannot exclude the other from the matrimonial home. This principle applies whether the matrimonial home is owned, rented or let on a contractual licence (section 1(1) of the Matrimonial Homes Act 1983). Similarly, a spouse who has been wrongfully evicted or excluded from the matrimonial home may by court order be allowed to re-enter.

If the tenant leaves, the landlord, licensor or mortgagee is obliged to accept payments (of rent, licence fees or mortgage repayments) as if the payments were made by the tenant (section 1(5) of the 1983 Act). Thus, the spouse is able to keep a tenancy alive even if abandoned by his or her partner. The court also has the power to transfer a tenancy from one spouse's name into the other's (section 7 of and Schedule 1 to the Matrimonial Homes Act). This power applies to both assured and secure tenancies. If divorce proceedings have been started, it is essential that the tenant applies to the court for such an order before the decree absolute.

Rights of remaining spouse

It should also be noted that if a possession order has been made against the tenant, the tenant's spouse, provided he or she is still living in the property, has the same rights to apply to the court to postpone suspend or vary the terms of the order (see chapter 11).

Trespassers

Persons in occupation of property without the landlord's permission fall into two main categories: people who have entered into possession without the permission of the owner (squatters or trespassers), and people who entered with the owner's permission (licensees). The distinction is an important one.

Licensees

Although a licensee who has had his or her licence revoked is technically a trespasser, the landlord is obliged to serve a notice to quit in the prescribed form, and will need a court order to ensure the licensee's eviction.

Squatters and trespassers

A person who enters another's premises without any licence to do so is a trespasser and, as long as violence is not used, the landlord may simply remove that person from the premises, or wait until they have left and then change the locks to ensure they cannot re-enter. In practice, such are the risks inherent in acting in this way that it is common to seek a court order.

County court procedure

Order 24 of the County Court Rules provides a swift way of obtaining possession against former licensees or tres-passers. The only difficulty for the landlord arises if the occupier is able to attend court and argue that he or she is, in fact, a tenant holding over.

Hostels

Those who live in hostels have already been considered briefly in this book. In this chapter the various aspects of the security that a hostel dweller may enjoy are shown together. Three principal factors will determine whether or not there is any security:

● whether the landlord falls under the Housing Act 1985 or the Housing Act 1988;

● whether the occupier has a tenancy agreement or a licence;

● whether the occupier shares living accommodation with other occupiers.

Housing Act 1985

Those landlords which are potentially secure landlords under the 1985 Act are identified in chapter 3. If the landlord fulfils the landlord condition, it is then necessary to examine whether the occupier fulfils the conditions necessary to be a secure tenant or licensee.

Tenancy or licence?

The Housing Act 1985 applies to both tenancies and licences (section 79(1),(3)). It has been held, however, that for a licence to be secure it must also, in effect, grant the occupier exclusive possession of the premises (see further chapter 2, and *Westminster City Council v Clarke* (1992), the details of which are set out in that chapter). Thus, for example, an agreement which genuinely reserves to the landlord the right to move the occupier to another room, will not create the type of licence which can potentially be secure, and the occupier will have no security of tenure.

Shared living accommodation

Where the occupier has a tenancy or exclusive licence of hostel accommodation, he or she will still not be secure if any living accommodation is shared. This is because of the requirement in section 79(1) of the Housing Act 1985 that the accommodation is let as a separate dwelling (see chapter 4). Thus, shared kitchens will take the occupation outside the protection of the Act. If, however, all the necessary requirements for sleeping, cooking and feeding are provided within the occupier's own exclusive accommodation, he or she will be a secure tenant or licensee.

Housing Act 1988

Where the landlord is, say a housing association, and lets hostel accommodation under the Housing Act 1988, it is possible for the occupiers to be assured.

Tenancy or licence?

The agreement with the occupier must grant a tenancy since the Housing Act 1988 does not apply to licences (see chapter 4). So again, as with the Housing Act 1985, a genuine licence agreement (see chapter 2) will not qualify for the protection of the 1988 Act.

Shared living accommodation

Unlike the position under the 1985 Act, however, sharing living accommodation with other residents will not prevent the letting being assured (section 3 of the 1988 Act; see chapter 4). Thus, if the occupier is granted a tenancy of a room in a hostel, and shares a kitchen, the letting will be assured.

Assured shorthold lettings

Where a landlord is granting tenancies to hostel occupiers, but wishes to maintain some flexibility about obtaining possession, there is no reason why the letting should not be an assured shorthold (see chapter 10).

Examples

> A borough council owns a hostel which is occupied by single homeless people. Each occupier has a room, but there are shared kitchens — one kitchen for every six occupiers. The occupiers sign a licence agreement, which reserves the right to the council to move occupiers to different rooms for management reasons. The council also provides cleaners, who enter the rooms three times a week to clean, and permanent support staff in the hostel. The occupiers are not secure, first because the agreements are licences which do not provide exclusive possession; and secondly, even if exclusive possession was granted the occupiers share living accommodation and therefore cannot be secure.

> A housing association owns a hostel for young single mothers. There are five bedsitting rooms in the hostel, but none has cooking facilities. A shared kitchen is provided. All the residents moved in after 15 January, 1989. All signed agreements, which purport to grant only licences to the occupiers of the rooms. No rights to move the occupiers are reserved by the licence, nor are any facilities provided which entail access to the rooms. The housing association has a key to each room, and provides some support workers, who visit the hostel regularly. There may be some basis for arguing that the licences are not genuine and that each resident has a tenancy (see chapter 2 and *FHA v Jones* (1989) 22 HLR 45 CA). If the residents have tenancies, then they will be assured. The fact that there is shared living accommodation will not prevent the lettings from being assured (section 3 of the Housing Act 1988).

Gaining possession

Where a secure or assured tenancy has been granted, then possession must be obtained in one of the ways set out in chapter 5. The proper procedures must be observed, and unless the letting is an assured shorthold (see chapter 10), then a ground will have to be proved against the occupier.

Excluded tenancy or licence

Where, however, there is no security of tenure, the hostel occupier who occupies under a licence, will generally have even fewer rights than others with limited security. Although the requirements of a notice to quit (section 5 of the Protection from Eviction Act 1977) and a court order (section 3 of that Act) set out in chapter 10, generally apply to licences as well as to tenancies, they do not apply where the tenancy or licence is 'excluded.' By section 3A(9) of the Protection from Eviction Act 1977 a licence (but not a tenancy) is excluded where it is granted by one of a number of public sector landlords (including local authorities, charitable housing trusts and registered housing associations) and confers the right of occupation in a hostel.

'Hostel' for these purposes is defined by section 622 of the Housing Act 1985 as:

> 'a building in which is provided for persons generally or for a class or classes of persons:
> (a) residential accommodation otherwise than in separate and self-contained sets of premises, and
> (b) either board or facilities for the preparation of food adequate to the needs of those persons, or both.'

Notice

If an occupier of hostel accommodation has a licence to occupy, then he or she essentially has the right only to such period of notice as may be specified in the licence agreement or, if no notice period is specified, reasonable notice. In the case of, say, dangerous or offensive behaviour by the hostel occupier it may be reasonable to give notice to leave immediately. Provided no violence is used, such an occupier may then be evicted on the spot.

CHAPTER 11

POSSESSION ORDERS

Once the court has decided that a ground for possession is made out, and that, if necessary, it is reasonable to make the order, and/or that suitable alternative accommodation is available, a possession order must be made. This does not mean that the landlord will be entitled to immediate possession of the property.

There are three types of possession order: immediate, outright, and suspended.

Immediate orders

Immediate orders allow the landlord to gain possession straightaway, although there will be a delay until the bailiff actually carries out the eviction. This sort of order is relevant only to the eviction of trespassers.

Outright order

The second type of order is an outright order which specifies a date in the future upon which the occupier must give up possession. The date is commonly 14 days after the court hearing. Landlords may agree to extend the period if there is no pressing need for possession. This will perhaps be the case if the occupiers have been living in the property for many years, or are undergoing hardship at the time of the hearing. In county court cases, the period may be extended to a maximum of 6 weeks (section 89 of the Housing Act 1980). Indeed, unless the landlord consents, the tenant may be granted a postponement of the order for longer than 14 days only if the tenant can demonstrate that such a short delay would cause 'exceptional hardship'. What constitutes exceptional hardship is unclear, but there must be circumstances over and above the normal consequences of being made homeless.

Suspended order

The court may instead make a suspended possession order, under which the operation of the order is suspended so long as the tenant complies with certain terms or conditions. These may include paying the current rent, and a weekly or monthly, sum off the arrears, or not committing any further nuisance or annoyance to neighbours. Almost all rent arrears cases result in suspended possession orders.

Powers of the court

The powers of the court to impose terms are very wide. Section 85 of Housing Act 1985 and section 9 of the

Housing Act 1988 set out the court's powers to adjourn proceedings, or to stay or suspend the execution of an order for possession. These powers are available only when possession is sought under one of the discretionary grounds (grounds 1–8 and 12–16 under the 1985 Act and grounds 9–16 under the 1988 Act).

Terms

The court may not suspend the order on terms which are unreasonable or would cause exceptional hardship. In rent arrears cases, if the tenant receives income support and a suspended possession order is made, the weekly amount which the tenant will be ordered to pay to reduce the rent arrears will be very small. Generally, it is the same as that which the DSS usually deducts from a tenant's entitlement to income support when the claimant is in arrears of rent. For the financial year 1995-1996 this figure is £2.30. If the arrears are high, it may take years to pay them off. Although swift payment of arrears may not be achieved, suspended possession orders usually require the tenant to continue paying the current rent, which should at least ensure that the tenant does not default again.

Spouses

A spouse of a tenant has the same rights as the tenant to seek the suspension or postponement of orders, as long as the spouse is still living in the premises.

Varying the terms

The tenant is entitled to make further applications if there is difficulty in complying with the terms of the suspended order. The court has the power to vary orders as it thinks fit. But, if the tenant fails to keep up with payments, that will not always be the last chance to stay in the property.

Discharge

If the conditions of the order are complied with, then the court may discharge the order.

Warrant for possession

Otherwise, as soon as the tenant is in breach of the terms of the order, the landlord may apply to the court for a warrant for possession. The landlord is under no obligation to notify the tenant that this action is being taken. Normally, the landlord will give the tenant some opportunity to explain the default, and make late payment.

Loss of secure tenancy

Defaulting on payment is of particular significance to a secure tenant. Once the terms of the order are breached, the order takes effect with the result that the tenant is no longer secure. This will mean that the tenant will lose all the additional rights, such as the right to buy, which a secure tenant has. The tenant may still apply to the court to vary the order, or to suspend execution of the warrant for possession, but the secure tenancy will not be revived by a successful application. While section 85 of the Housing Act 1985 provides an added safeguard against eviction, it does not affect the legal consequences of a possession order against a secure tenant.

Example

Mr and Mrs Thompson were married in 1983. In 1984 Mrs Thompson was granted a secure tenancy by a local authority. Arrears of rent accrued, and in January 1985 the local authority obtained a possession order against Mrs Thompson suspended on terms that she paid the current rent plus £10 a week off the arrears. The terms of the order were breached. In January 1986 the local authority obtained a warrant for possession. In February 1986 Mr Thompson applied to the court to be added to the possession action, for a declaration that he had a right to occupy the matrimonial home, and for the warrant of possession to be suspended. The judge dismissed his applications, and the Court of Appeal upheld the judge's decision. It was held that once there was a breach of the terms of a suspended possession order the secure tenancy determined. The subsequent applications were therefore misconceived (*Thompson v Elmbridge Borough Council* (1987) 19 HLR 526 CA).

Acceptance of rent

Tenants sometimes argue that a new tenancy has been created by the acceptance of rent by the landlord after some act which would normally indicate that the old tenancy is at an end. This often occurs because one department collects the rent, and another has the day-to-day management of the premises. Although the payment of rent, by reference to a term, by someone with exclusive possession of premises normally denotes a tenancy, where there has been a dispute between the parties, the landlord will be able to argue that there was no intention to create legal relations, with the consequence that no new tenancy was created (see chapter 2).

Application to set aside

Even after the execution of the warrant for possession, it is not too late for the tenant to apply to the court. At this stage the Housing Acts are of no avail, but the tenant, may nevertheless apply under Order 37 of the County Court Rules. Rule 2 of Order 37 allows the court to set aside any order made in the tenant's absence. Under rule 3 a judgment may be set aside where there has been a failure of the postal service and notice of any hearing did not come to the tenant's attention in time. Rule 5 gives the court discretion to set aside any judgment where there has been a failure to comply with the court rules. It is also possible to apply to the court for a rehearing where there has been misconduct by the plaintiff, or where fresh evidence has come to light.

Although the tenant may apply under Order 37 after execution of the warrant, the application is unlikely to succeed if there has been a long delay in applying, and the landlord would be prejudiced were the application to succeed. If an order is set aside the landlord will have to allow the tenant back into the property. Accordingly, whether or not the property has been re-let is a key factor.

Example

> Mr Khan went abroad in February 1978. He made no arrangements for the rent to be paid whilst he was away. He returned in July 1979 to find that a possession order had been made against him in May 1979. The property had been re-let. He applied to set aside the order. His application was refused. The court said that his prolonged absence, and the high level of rent arrears would lead any reasonable landlord to believe that the tenant had abandoned the property. Furthermore, the property had been re-let, and it was necessary to balance the rights of the new tenant against those of the former tenant (*Rhodes Trust v Khan* (1979) SJ 719).

CHAPTER 12

TERMINATION BY THE TENANT

The tenant, rather than the landlord, may wish to terminate the tenancy. The two ways in which this may be
achieved are by surrender, and by notice to quit.

Surrender

Surrender is a way in which a tenant, with the agreement
of the landlord, may bring a tenancy to an end. The tenant
may surrender a tenancy whether it is fixed term or
periodic.

Agreement to surrender

Surrender is in effect an agreement between the landlord
and the tenant to bring the tenancy to an end. The tenant
cannot force the landlord to agree. Technically, surrender
should take place by the drawing up of a formal deed, but
this is rare.

By operation of law

Surrender can also take place by operation of law, when the tenant does an unequivocal act which is inconsistent with the continuation of the tenancy, and the landlord accepts the act of the tenant as surrender of the tenancy. The most common example is the delivery of the keys to the landlord with the intention of bringing the tenancy to an end.

Surrender may also take place if the tenant abandons the premises. Although the landlord may wish to argue that surrender has in fact taken place in such circumstances great care must be taken in deciding whether or not that is truly the case. The tenant may be absent because of illness, or away on business, but may still intend to return. If this is so, and the landlord mistakenly assumes the tenant has abandoned the premises and takes back possession the landlord may be liable in damages for unlawfully evicting the tenant. This aspect of surrender is further considered in chapter 4.

Surrender by joint tenants

If the tenancy is a joint tenancy all the joint tenants must agree to the surrender.

Examples

> Mrs Toth was granted a secure tenancy by Croydon Borough Council in August 1981. She married in March 1982, and in October 1982 a child was born. Substantial rent arrears had accrued and in May 1982 a suspended order for possession was granted. In November 1982 the DSS began to pay the rent directly to the council.
>
> Towards the end of August 1983, Mrs Toth's husband left her, and she did not see him again. A few days later, four men appeared and demanded to see her husband, saying that he owed them £1200. At that time he was

wanted by the police for robbery. She told the men that he had left. They replied that if she did not have the money by the next Friday they would harm her and the baby.

As a result she left the premises taking with her what belongings she could and putting the rest in the garage. She lived at first as a squatter, and when that property was repossessed she moved in with her sister. She eventually applied as homeless to the council. In the meantime the council had been informed by her neighbours in September 1993 that the occupants of the premises had moved out. The council inspected the property and found this to be correct. The locks were changed and it was assumed that the premises were abandoned. The premises were re-let in October 1983.

On a challenge to the council's decision that she was intentionally homeless, one of the issues was whether Mrs Toth had moved out temporarily, or whether she had in fact surrendered her tenancy. The Court of Appeal held that there had been a surrender by operation of law. There was overwhelming evidence that the tenant had given possession and that the landlord had accepted this by changing the locks and re-letting the premises. Her subsequent assertion that she had no intention of leaving permanently was not relevant (*R v London Borough of Croydon ex p Toth* (1987) 20 HLR 576).

Mr Sharma was granted a secure tenancy in 1984 by Brent Borough Council. His partner lived with him from time to time, and they had two children. In January 1987 Mr Sharma moved out of the flat and surrendered his tenancy. The council granted a tenancy of the flat to the partner. She later moved out, to another area where she was granted a secure tenancy. Mr Sharma returned to the flat and lived there with two children from a previous relationship.

In November 1988 his former partner wrote to the

council stating that she was no longer sharing the flat, and had no objection to it being transferred to Mr Sharma who continued to live there. At this stage there were arrears of over £4000. The council served an ineffective notice to quit in September 1989. Possession was sought in September 1989, and granted on the basis that there had been an effective surrender. The Court of Appeal upheld this decision. There was an unequivocal act by the former partner in writing to the council and that this was unequivocally accepted by the council was shown by the fact that they no longer charged any rent to her and had served the notice to quit (*London Borough of Brent v Sharma* (1992) 25 HLR 257).

Notice to quit

A tenant may determine the tenancy by giving the landlord a valid notice to quit. This method of termination is available only to periodic tenants. Unlike surrender, the landlord's compliance is not necessary. The notice must be in writing, but there is no prescribed form.

Contents
Contents must state the date on which the tenancy is to determine, and the notice must be given at least four weeks before that date. A monthly tenancy requires a month's notice, a quarterly tenancy a quarter's notice, and a yearly tenancy six months' notice. The notice should be made to expire on the last day of the period of the tenancy.

Joint tenants
Unlike surrender, it is not necessary for all the joint tenants to agree for the tenancy to be determined by a tenant's notice to quit.

Effect

Once the notice to quit has expired the tenant ceases to have any rights as a secure or assured tenant. Even if the tenant changes his or her mind the landlord can proceed to evict, although the landlord is not, of course, bound so to do and may choose instead to grant a new tenancy to the tenant.

Joint tenants

What happens when only one of two joint tenants wishes to leave the property? If one abandons it, the remaining joint tenant becomes the sole tenant. The position is more complicated when one of the tenants tries to terminate the tenancy by a notice to quit or surrender. As noted above, all the joints tenants must agree for the tenancy to be terminated by surrender. One joint tenant alone is capable of terminating the contractual tenancy by notice to quit (*Hammersmith London Borough Council v Monk* [1992] 1 AC 478 HL). This can be of great use to a tenant who has been excluded from the home by a violent joint tenant, and is helpful to local authorities and housing associations dealing with domestic breakdown. Where, for example, a husband has been left in the family home and the landlord wishes to rehouse the wife and children, the wife can be asked to serve a notice to quit. This enables the landlord to evict the husband, freeing the accommodation for re-letting to a family, while the wife is rehoused elsewhere.

Any notice to quit served by the tenant must, however, comply with the common law requirements of notice to quit and those in section 5 of the Protection from Eviction Act 1977 (see chapter 10).

Example

In 1991 Hounslow borough council granted a joint tenancy to Mr Pilling and his partner. The tenancy agreement provided for termination by the tenant by giving four weeks' written notice 'or such lesser period as the council may accept'. In September 1991, following incidents of domestic violence, Mr Pilling's partner left the premises permanently. To obtain alternative housing from the council under their rehousing policy, she wrote to the council stating that: 'I wish to terminate my tenancy . . . with immediate effect'. Following receipt of this letter the council wrote to Mr Pilling stating that his tenancy had been terminated and sought possession.

In the Court of Appeal it was held that the notice given by Mr Pilling's partner was not valid to terminate the tenancy. To terminate a joint tenancy the notice must be appropriate, which means it must comply with the requirements of common law and with section 5 of the Protection from Eviction Act 1977 (*London Borough of Hounslow v Pilling* (1993) 25 HLR 305).

APPENDIX

SPECIMEN LETTERS AND FORMS

1. Letter to illegal occupier

[Landlord's address]

Dear Ms Tomlinson, [date]

Following our meeting with you on [*date*], we write to confirm our position concerning your occupation of [*address of premises*]. We are the landlord of this flat. You have no agreement with us. The tenant is Mr Quade. You explained that Mr Quade left the flat some time before [*date*] [*or* you pay a weekly rent of £x to Mr Quade and he has not lived at the flat since you began living there on (*date*)] [*or* you say that Mr Quade is currently travelling and he has allowed you to live in the flat while he is away]. Our investigations show that Mr Quade now lives at [*new principal home*].

A notice to quit requiring possession of the flat has been served determining the contractual tenancy with Mr Quade. We will commence possession proceedings when this notice has expired on [*date*]. Any money accepted from you by us will be accepted only as damages for your use and occupation of the premises pending the conclusion of the possession proceedings. The acceptance by us of such sums is not intended to create a tenancy between you and us.

Yours etc

2. Letter to tenant with rent arrears

Dear Ms Tenant,

I called at your home today order to discuss your rent account, but unfortunately you were out. Your weekly rent is £37.45. Your rent account shows that you are now £449.40 in arrears. This is wholly unacceptable.

Please telephone me as soon as possible [*number provided*] at any time between 2 pm and 4.30 pm, so we can discuss arrangements for clearing your account.

I must warn you that if you do not contact me within the next two weeks, the Council will take steps to recover the rent arrears and evict you from your home. I emphasise that we hope to reach an agreement, but unless you contact me the Council will be obliged to take the necessary steps.

Yours etc

3. Letter to tenant causing nuisance or annoyance

Dear Mr Tenant,

I have received complaints from your neighbours. They say that you play your stereo very loudly, particularly late at night, and that you are constantly having large numbers of visitors at all hours of the night. It is also said that you make no effort to keep the noise down when requested by your neighbours. I have been informed that, in the early hours of Sunday 29 October 1994, the police were called to your flat because of the noise.

Of course, no one objects to your playing your stereo, and having guests, but it is quite unacceptable to disturb your neighbours. I refer you to clause [*clause number*] of your tenancy agreement which specifically states that you are not to cause a nuisance to your neighbours. If you continue to act in a way which shows no regard for your neighbours the Housing Association may take proceedings against you to evict you from your home.

It is clearly in everybody's best interests for you to ensure that there are no further disturbances of this nature. I thank you in expectation of your cooperation.

Yours etc

4. Letter to tenants whose home is to be redeveloped

Dear Mr and Mrs Tenant,

As you know, the Council intends to carry out extensive works of modernisation to your home. The Council surveyor believes that the works cannot be carried out while you and your family are living in the house. I have already written to you telling you that a three-bedroomed house, 4 Blythe Drive, London E 27, is available for you to move into while the contractors are working on your home. I have been informed that you told Ms Summerson, our housing officer, that you had no intention of moving, and have refused to view 4 Blythe Drive.

I must emphasise that it is absolutely necessary that you move before works commence. Please contact me to arrange to see 4 Blythe Drive, which is similar to your own house. I must warn you that if you do not cooperate the Council will have no choice but to take proceedings to evict you, in which case you may have to pay the Council's costs.

I stress that the Council prefers not have to take such action, and remind you that the works which are to be carried out will be of great benefit to you on your return.

Yours etc

5. Notice seeking possession from a secure tenant

Words shown in italic type are the instructions for completion which are given in the statutory form. Words in square brackets have been added here to show how the notice might look when completed.

HOUSING ACT 1985

Section 83

Notice of Seeking Possession
This notice is the first step towards requiring you to give up possession of your dwelling. You should read it carefully.

1. To (*names of secure tenant(s)*):
                    [Arnold Tenant]
                    [Miriam Tenant]

If you need advice about this notice, and what you should do about it, take it as quickly as possible to a Citizen's Advice Bureau, a Housing Aid Centre, or a Law Centre, or to a solicitor. You may be able to receive Legal Aid but this will depend on your personal circumstances.

2. The (*name of landlord*) [London Borough of Finsbury] intends to apply to the Court for an order requiring you to give up possession of (*address of property*)

[72 Lamb Park Estate,
Harvey Road,
London N34 9QT]

If you are a secure tenant under the Housing Act 1985, you can only be required to leave your dwelling if your landlord obtains an order for possession from the Court. The order must be based on one of the Grounds which are set out in the Housing Act 1985 (see paragraphs 3 and 4 below).

If you are willing to give up possession without a court order, you should notify the person who gave you this Notice as soon as possible and say when you would leave.

3. Possession will be sought on (*give the text in full of each Ground which is being relied upon*) Grounds 1 and 3 of Schedule 2 to the Housing Act 1985 which read:
[GROUND 1:
Rent lawfully due from the tenant has not been paid or an obligation of the tenancy has been broken or not performed.]
[GROUND 3:
The condition of the dwelling house or any of the common parts has deteriorated owing to acts of waste by, or the neglect of, the tenant or a person residing in the dwelling house and, in the case of an act of waste by, or

the neglect or default of, a person lodging with the tenant or a subtenant of his, the tenant has not taken such steps as he ought reasonably to have taken for the removal of the lodger or subtenant.]

Whatever Grounds for possession are set out in paragraph 4 of this Notice, the Court may allow any of the other grounds to be added at a later stage. If this is done, you will be told about it so you can argue at the hearing in the Court about the new Ground, as well as the Grounds set out in paragraph 3, if you want to.

4. (*Give a full explanation of why each Ground is being relied upon*). Particulars of each ground are as follows:
[GROUND 1:
Under the terms of the tenancy agreement the tenants are required to pay rent of £34.50 per week. As of today's date the arrears of rent owed by the tenants amount to £743.50.]
[GROUND 2:
Owing to acts of neglect or default of the tenants the condition of the dwelling house has deteriorated. Without prejudice to the generality of the foregoing, the windows in the dwelling have been broken, the front door has been damaged and the bath and WC have become stained and insanitary.

Further owing to acts of vandalism committed by Mr Arnold Tenant on or about 12 February 1994 the communal lift in the block no longer functions.]

Before the Court will grant an order on any of the Grounds 1 to 8 or 12 to 16, it must be satisfied that it is reasonable to require you to leave. This means that, if one of these Grounds is set out in paragraph 3 of this notice you will be able to argue at the hearing in Court that it is not reasonable that you should have to leave, even if you accept that the Ground applies.

Before the Court grants an order on any of the Grounds 9 to 16, it must be satisfied that there will be suitable alternative accommodation for you when you have to leave. This means that the Court will have to decide that, in its opinion, there will be other accommodation which is reasonably suitable for the needs of you and your family, taking into particular account various factors such as the nearness of your place of work, and the sort of housing that other people with similar needs are offered. Your new home will have to be let to you on another secure tenancy or a private tenancy under the Rent Act of a kind that will give you similar security. There is no requirement for suitable alternative accommodation where Grounds 1 to 8 apply.

If your landlord is not a local authority, and the local authority gives a certificate that it will provide you with suitable accommodation, the Court has to accept that certificate.

One of the requirements of Ground 10A is that the landlord must have approval for the redevelopment scheme from the Secretary of State (or, in the case of a housing association landlord, the Housing Corporation). The landlord must have consulted all secure tenants affected by the proposed redevelopment scheme.

5. The Court proceedings will not be begun until after (*Give the date after which Court proceedings can be brought*) [31 March 1995].

Court proceedings cannot be begun until after this date, which cannot be earlier than the date when your tenancy or licence could have been brought to an end. This means that if you have a weekly or fortnightly tenancy, there should be at least 4 weeks between the date this notice is given and the date in this paragraph.

After this date, court proceedings may be begun at once or at any time during the following twelve months.

Once the twelve months are up this notice will lapse and a new notice must be served before possession can be sought.

Signed: Christopher Marlow
On behalf of the London Borough of Finsbury
Address: Finsbury Town Hall
The Melon Road
London NW34 6NP
Tel No: 081 123 4567
Date: 27 February 1995

6. Notice seeking possession from an assured tenant

Words shown in italic type are the instructions for completion which are given in the statutory form. Words in square brackets have been added here to show how the notice might look when completed.

HOUSING ACT 1988

Section 8

Notice of seeking possession of a property let on an assured tenancy

- Please write clearly in black ink
- Do not use this form if possession is sought from an assured shorthold tenant under section 21 of the Housing Act 1988 or if the property is occupied under an assured agricultural occupancy.
- This notice is the first step towards requiring you to give up possession of your home. You should read it very carefully.

If you need advice about this notice, and what you should do about it, take it as quickly as possible to any of the following—
- a Citizens' Advice Bureau
- a Housing Aid Centre
- a Law Centre
- or a Solicitor.

You may be able to get Legal Aid but this will depend on your personal circumstances.

1. To: (*Name of tenant*) [Mark Trevor Andrewes]

2. Your landlord intends to apply to the Court for an order requiring you to give up possession of (*Address of premises*):

[13 Severin House,
Marine Road,
Middleton,
Wessex WI5 6PW.]

•   If you have an assured tenancy under the Housing Act 1988, which is not an assured shorthold tenancy, you can only be required to leave your home if your landlord gets an order for possession from the Court on one of the grounds which are set out in Schedule 2 to the Housing Act 1988.

•   If you are willing to give up possesion of your home without a court order, you should tell the person who signed this notice as soon as possible and say when you can leave.

3. The landlord intends to seek possession on Grounds [12 and 14] in Schedule 2 to the Housing Act 1988 which read: (*Give the full text of each ground which is being relied upon. Continue on a separate sheet if necessary.*)

[GROUND 12:
Any obligation of the tenancy (other than one related to the payment of rent) has been broken or not performed.]
[GROUND 14:
The tenant or other person residing in the dwelling house has been guilty of conduct which is a nuisance or annoyance to adjoining occupiers, or has been convicted of using the dwelling house or allowing the dwelling house to be used for immoral or illegal purposes.]

• Whichever Grounds are set out in paragraph 3 the court may allow any of the other Grounds to be added at a later date. If this is done, you will be told about it so you can discuss the additional Grounds at the court hearing as well as the Grounds set out in paragraph 3.

4. The particulars of each Ground are as follows: (*Give a full explanation of why each Ground is being relied on. Continue on a separate sheet if necessary.*)
[GROUND 12:
    (a) In breach of clause 3(2) of the tenancy agreement, under which the tenant covenants not to keep any animal or pet on the premises, the tenant keeps two dogs in the dwelling.
    (b) In breach of clause 3(4) of the tenancy agreement, under which the tenant covenants not to cause any nuisance or annoyance to adjoining occupiers, the tenant has caused nuisance and annoyance to his adjoining occupiers. Particulars of the alleged acts of nuisance are contained under Ground 14 below.]
[GROUND 14:
The tenant has been guilty of causing nuisance and annoyance to his adjoining occupiers.
    (a) The tenant allows his dogs freely to roam about the common parts and foul the communal walkways;
    (b) On three or four nights each week the tenant plays his stereo radio or television after 11 pm at such a vol-

ume that his neighbours are unable to sleep or enjoy the use of their homes;

(c) On four occasions in the last five months, on 21 July 1994, 3 August 1994, 7 November 1994, and 18 November 1994 the tenant has caused or allowed his bath to overflow causing flooding to flat 21 which is situated directly below the premises.]

• If the court is satisfied that any of Grounds 1 to 8 is established it must make an order (but see below in respect of fixed term tenancies).

• Before the court will grant an order on any of Grounds 9 to 16, it must be satisfied that it is reasonable to require you to leave. This means that, if one of these Grounds is set out in paragraph 3, you will be able to suggest to the court that it is not reasonable that you should have to leave, even if you accept that the Ground applies.

• The court will not make an order under Grounds 1, 3 to 7, 9 or 16 to take effect during the fixed term of the tenancy; and it will only make an order during the fixed term on Grounds 2, 8, or 10 to 15 if the terms of the tenancy make provision for it to be brought to an end on any of these Grounds.

• Where the court makes an order for possession solely on Ground 6 or 9, your landlord must pay your reasonable removal expenses.

5. The court proceedings will not begin until after (*Give the date after which court proceedings can be brought.*) [17 February 1995].

• Where the landlord or licensor is seeking possession under Grounds 1, 2, 5 to 7, 9 or 16 in Schedule 2, court proceedings cannot be begun earlier than 2 months from the date this notice is served on you and not before the date on which the tenancy (had it not been assured) could have been brought to an end by a notice to quit served at the same time as this notice.

• Where the landlord is seeking possession on Grounds 3, 4, 8 or 10 to 15, court proceedings cannot begin until 2 weeks after the date this notice is served.

• After the date shown in paragraph 5, court proceedings may be begun at once but not later than 12 months from the date this notice is served. After this time the notice will lapse and a new notice must be served before possession can be sought.

(To be signed by the landlord or their servant or their agent).
[Signed: Bertha Johnstone
Landlord: Westland Housing Association
Address: 83 Carroway Street
Livesey
Wessex W2 7NY
Tel No: 5674 9898]
Date: 16 January 1995

7. Notice to quit

Notice to quit

To Mr John Brown of 41 Ilsham Road London NW19 6FH

I on behalf of your landlord, the Marine Housing Association of 67 Kent St, London NW19 8GH give you NOTICE TO QUIT and deliver up possession to the Marine Housing Association of 41 Ilsham Road London NW19 6FH on 14 November 1994, or the day on which a complete period of your tenancy expires next after the end of four weeks from the service of this notice.

Dated 12 October 1994
Signed Jonathan Murray

Information for tenant

1. If the tenant or licensee does not leave the dwelling, the landlord or licensor must get an order for possession from the court before the tenant or licensee can lawfully be evicted. The landlord or licensor cannot apply for such an order before the notice to determine has run out.

2. A tenant or licensee who does not know if he has any right to remain in possession after a notice to quit or a notice to determine runs out can obtain advice from a solicitor. Help with all or part of the cost of legal advice and assistance may be available under the legal aid scheme. He should also be able to obtain information from a Citizens' Advice Bureau, a Housing Aid Centre or a rent officer.

8. Diary of incidents form

Name of witness: —————————————————
Address of witness: ————————————————
Name of tenant against whom complaints are made:
Address of tenant: ————————————————
Please complete this form for a period of one month, keeping a record of each incident of nuisance or annoyance which you experience. Please remember that tenants are expected to have to endure a certain amount of noise etc from their neighbours, so please do not record incidents which are insignificant.

Date	Time started	Time finished	Nuisance complained of *ie, noise, smell, etc, indicating the source of the nuisance, eg, for noise: shouting, television, working noises, or parties.*

GLOSSARY OF TERMS

This glossary provides a concise explanation of the meaning of some of the more legalistic and technical terms used in the guide.

Assured tenancy
– a tenancy that fulfils the requirements of the Housing Act 1988. An assured tenancy can be granted only from 15 January 1989 by landlords who are either housing associations or in the private sector.

Common law
– a phrase generally used to describe the law arising not from statutory sources but from case-law.

Covenant
– a clause in a tenancy agreement under which either the landlord or tenant promises to act in a certain way, for

example, to carry out repairs, or not to be a nuisance to neighbours.

Ex parte
– an application to the court, which is made urgently and without the opposing party in the litigation being informed that the hearing is to take place. (Abbreviation: *ex p.*)

Fixed term tenancy
– a tenancy which is granted for a fixed period, for example, six months, or one year, or 99 years. (Compare *Periodic tenancy*, below.)

Injunction
– an order of the court that a person should carry out certain acts or should refrain from carrying out certain acts.

Interlocutory
– an interim order in a case that is made before the final trial and judgment, most often used with injunctions.

Nuisance
– the interference by one occupier of land with other's occupation of their own land.

Periodic tenancy
– a tenancy which does not have a fixed time-span from the outset, but which is set in terms of a regular rental payment, for example, monthly or weekly.

Quiet enjoyment
– the right of tenants to occupy their homes without interference from their landlords. A right to quiet

enjoyment is automatically implied into all tenancy agreements.

Secure tenancy
– a tenancy that fulfils the requirements of the Housing Act 1985, granted by local authorities, or, before 15 January 1989, housing associations.

Specific performance
– an order of the court that a particular term of a contract should be performed, for example, to carry out repairs; or to desist from behaviour which is a breach of a tenancy agreement.

INDEX

Arden's Housing Library

Law and practice in the management of social housing
Series Editors: Andrew Arden,QC and Caroline Hunter

There is a legal foundation underpinning almost every decision taken by housing managers. The books in Arden's Housing Library explain those foundations and ensure that the legal framework, implications and possibilities of day-to-day housing management are fully understood and can be translated into good practice.

Andrew Arden,QC and Caroline Hunter are the Series Editors of Arden's Housing Library. They are also the joint editors of the *Housing Law Reports* and the *Encyclopedia of Housing Law and Practice*. Andrew Arden,QC is widely regarded as the leading expert on housing law and local government law and procedure. He has conducted major inquiries into local councils and housing associations. Caroline Hunter is a barrister and lecturer in law at Nottingham University.

Books in Arden's Housing Library published simultaneously:
Vol 1: Security of Tenure and *Vol 2: Tenants' Rights*.

Tenants' Rights
Vol. 2 of Arden's Housing Library
by Caroline Hunter

Tenants' rights are a new area of law. Beginning in 1980, these rights have been swiftly developed and expanded. Secure tenants of councils and housing associations now have more control over their homes than ever before. So keeping abreast of tenants' rights is now essential for anyone working in the housing field – and this book is the way to do it.

As individuals, many tenants may now take in lodgers, exchange their homes or even sublet them. Often other family members can succeed to a tenancy. Collectively tenants have new rights to information, to manage their own homes and even to change their landlord.

Tenants' rights is not always simple and it rarely applies equally to assured and secure tenants. This book is the only comprehensive summary of that law. Drawing heavily on examples from recent cases, *Tenants' Rights* is presented clearly and concisely – accessible to housing professionals and tenants alike.

About the author
Caroline Hunter is a barrister and lecturer in law at Nottingham University. She is joint series editor of *Arden's Housing Library* and joint editor of the *Housing Law Reports* and the *Encyclopedia of Housing Law and Practice*. She has written several books on housing law, including with (Andrew Arden,QC) *Manual of Housing Law* (5th edition), and (with Siobhan McGrath) *Homeless Persons: Arden's guide to the Housing Act 1985 Part III* (4th edition) and *Quiet Enjoyment* (4th edition). After working as an adviser for SHAC (the London Housing Aid Centre), Caroline Hunter practised for several years as a barrister, specialising in housing work. She has been extensively involved in teaching housing law to housing professionals.

Other housing books from Lemos

INTERVIEWING PERPETRATORS OF
RACIAL HARASSMENT
A Guide for Housing Managers
by Gerard Lemos

This is the first handbook for housing professionals giving
practical advice on how to interview perpetrators and stop
racial harassment. The guide focuses on stopping harassment early, before legal action is necessary. It contains
model documentation for day-to-day use in casework.
Interviewing Perpetrators of Racial Harassment is endorsed by
both the Chartered Institute of Housing and the Housing
Corporation.

"No area office should be without a copy." *Housing*

"The book is highly recommended." *HARUNews*